Thomas Henry Huxley, Samuel Laing

Pre-Historic Remains of Caithness

Thomas Henry Huxley, Samuel Laing

Pre-Historic Remains of Caithness

ISBN/EAN: 9783337366001

Printed in Europe, USA, Canada, Australia, Japan

Cover: Foto ©ninafisch / pixelio.de

More available books at **www.hansebooks.com**

PRE-HISTORIC REMAINS

OF

CAITHNESS,

BY

SAMUEL LAING, ESQ., M.P., F.G.S.

WITH

NOTES ON THE HUMAN REMAINS,

BY

THOMAS H. HUXLEY, ESQ., F.R.S.,
PROFESSOR OF NATURAL HISTORY, ROYAL SCHOOL OF MINES.

WILLIAMS AND NORGATE,
14, HENRIETTA STREET, COVENT GARDEN; AND
20, SOUTH FREDERICK STREET, EDINBURGH.
1866.

PRE-HISTORIC REMAINS

OF

CAITHNESS.

IN presenting to the Museum of Scottish Antiquaries the interesting series of Pre-historic Remains which I have had the good fortune to discover in Caithness, I think it desirable to place on record the principal facts connected with their discovery in a more complete form than was possible in the papers on the subject, which have been read at meetings of various learned Societies. I am further induced to adopt this course by the opportunity which it affords of giving illustrations of the objects for the benefit of those who may not have seen the originals, and more especially because it enables me to present to the scientific world the valuable remarks of Professor Huxley on the crania and skeletons, accompanied by accurate drawings which have been made under his superintendence.

A few introductory remarks may be permitted in order to explain the objects with which these researches were undertaken by me during a short residence in Caithness in the course of the past autumn.

The problem of British archæology may be thus stated. We know the two extremes of a series. The one is that of Quaternary man, whose relics have been found at Hoxne, in the drift gravels of the Ouse and Thames, the caves of

Torquay and the Mendips, and other localities. These clearly carry back the existence of man on British soil to a period contemporary with the flint weapons of Abbeville and Amiens, and with the river and cave-men of France and Germany; when very different conditions prevailed of climate, of sea and river-level, and of configuration of sea and land. At this period Britain was probably connected with the continent; the rigour of the glacial epoch had but partially abated; the great glacial rivers still poured forth volumes of muddy water into valleys in which the loëss was deposited which has since been excavated for hundreds of feet; the reindeer lived in the south of France; and the mammoth and woolly-haired rhinoceros roamed over the plains of what is now England.

In stating this as a fact, which by the mass of concurrent testimony is now placed beyond doubt, I offer no opinion as to the absolute antiquity of this period. That is a question for authorities who, like Lyell and Prestwich, have devoted their attention to "Quaternary Geology." If they are right in supposing that none but existing causes, or rather causes of the same order as those now existing, have brought about these changes, the period required is immense. But if, as some continental geologists believe, more intense and convulsive causes have prevailed, this period may be indefinitely shortened, for if we once depart from those operations of nature of which alone we have experience, all calculation becomes conjecture, and our chronological scale may as well be written in thousands as in tens of thousands of years. However, for archæological purposes this is a matter of indifference, and in either case we start with the fact that at the most remote period yet disclosed, when man existed on the continent along with the extinct animals, he also existed in Britain.

The other extreme of the series is defined by the first dawn of history, which shows us man existing in the British Isles with a knowledge of the metals and a certain amount of civilisation. From this point downwards archæology has so far explored the field that we can distinguish and classify an unbroken succession of the remains of the Keltic Britons; the Romans, and Romanized Britons; the Pagan and Christian Anglo-Saxons; and the Scandinavians; down to the Anglo-Norman and Mediæval periods where archæology ends.

The intermediate, or Secondary period, has, as regards the continent, been partially filled up by the result of researches into the Danish Kjökkenmöddings and Swiss Lacustrine-dwellings. The progression of a Stone, Bronze, and Iron period with different races of men, implements, and modes of sepulture, may be taken as established. In certain cases the distinctions may be a little doubtful, and the formations may, so to speak, overlap; yet on the whole there is evidence of a succession of races, and of a regular advance from rudeness to civilization and from lower to higher types of man.

In the case of the lowest Danish middens we are carried very far back in the scale both of time and civilization, and made acquainted with the race of the early Stone period who lived when the configuration of sea and land in Denmark was materially different; on a platform of fir forests which has been succeeded first by one of oak, and finally by that of beech, which alone is recorded in history; without a knowledge of the domestic animals, except the dog; and in a state of rudeness which argues little, if any, progress since the date of the quaternary men of Abbeville and Les Eyzies.

In Britain this Secondary period remains, however, in a state of great confusion. The fundamental distinction of a Stone, Bronze, and Iron period has never been either conclusively established or conclusively negatived. Every day we hear of relics which in Denmark would be assigned without hesitation to the Stone period, being found in connection with bronze and iron; and if the case rested solely on British evidence, probably most antiquarians would have been of opinion that there was no sufficient ground for any other hypothesis than that the race found in Britain by the Romans had colonized an unoccupied country a few centuries before the dawn of history. The utter uncertainty of what I have called the Archæology of the Secondary period in Britain is sufficiently shown by the speculations respecting the most important megalithic monument which we possess—that of Stonehenge—which has been assigned by different learned antiquaries with equal ingenuity and equal lack of solid arguments, to the era of Vortigern and Arthur; to that of Phœnician worship introduced in the flourishing days of Tyre and Tarshish; or finally, to the remote antiquity of some unknown Allophylian race.

The refuse heaps which have been the means of throwing so much light on the Pre-historic periods of Denmark and Switzerland appear to afford by far the best chance of ascertaining the habits and conditions of life of the pre-historic populations; but they require, even more than the ancient tombs and dwellings, the most accurate and systematic investigation, not only to give us truth, but to escape giving us error.

The shell-mound, or midden, is of itself a formation of no particular period. I have seen many a "Kjökkenmödding" accumulating at the back door of an Orkney cottage, where limpets were largely used for bait. It must be remembered also that the same mound has frequently been used over and over again for a succession of habitations.

There are many reasons why this must be the case, such as convenience of situation, access to the shore, drainage, supply of stones for building, and a richer soil and greener pasture; all of which are afforded to the new settler by the old ruined mound. In point of fact, very many cottages in Orkney and Caithness now stand on, or immediately adjoining to, old mounds; and a slight excavation, such as a child might make in sport, might readily bring together the contents of the recent and ancient middens, and place a halfpenny of Queen Victoria in juxtaposition with a stone celt or flint arrow. In my own limited explorations I have seen three or four instances which have taught me the necessity of extreme caution, and of attaching no weight whatever to the discovery of any article in connection with an old mound or building, which has not been found in some original undisturbed stratum, and its situation accurately noted at the time by a competent observer. In one case, a modern metal button was thrown up by the spade amidst débris of an ancient shell-midden. On investigation it was clearly proved to have been torn off the waistcoat of one of the workmen on the preceding day, and amidst a storm of wind and rain blown into and apparently incorporated with the refuse heap. Again, a coin of Elizabeth, which is now in my possession, was found in digging the foundation of a barn in Orkney, at about a foot below the surface, in a spot closely adjoining to a mound or Picts' house, some of the débris of which are at a level several feet higher than the site of the coin; so that if this estate were thrown into a large sheep farm, and the buildings removed, a century hence this coin might have been found in a green mound of shapeless ruins, at a level distinctly below stone hammers and teeth of *Bos longifrons*.

I dwell at some length on these instances, because I am convinced that nothing but error can result from attaching any weight to the evidence of simple juxtaposition in the same mound, refuse heap, or building, without accurate observation of the whole circumstances of each discovery; and, above all, that no reliance whatever is to be placed on anything which is found within two or three feet of the surface, in soil which is recent, or which may possibly have been disturbed.

As far as researches into the shell-middens of Scotland have hitherto extended, they have done little to clear up the uncertainty of British Pre-historic Archæology. Sir John

Lubbock, in the "Natural History Review" of July, 1863, gives a very interesting account of some which he visited in the neighbourhood of Elgin. He succeeded, however, only in finding shells, with fragments of bones of oxen, sheep, and pigs, and three small implements of bone. He remarks that the absence of pottery, and of implements either of flint, stone, or metal, is most "puzzling;" and he mentions that a bronze pin was shown him, said to have come from one of the mounds, the fashion of which showed it probably to be of quite recent date, or about A.D. 800 or 900.

Since the date of Sir John Lubbock's paper, Mr. Roberts has described, in the "Anthropological Review" of February, 1864, the result of his exploration of some shell-mounds, with associated cairns, at Bennet Hill, near Burghead. Two of the cairns covered rude stone kists, in one of which was found a complete skeleton, with a cranium of a decidedly brachycephalic type, of which a minute description is given by Mr. Busk. In the shell-mound nearest to the kist were found fragments of very rude pottery, and some flint arrow-heads.

Various incidental notices of refuse heaps of shells and bones are scattered throughout the numerous accounts of ancient tumuli, burgs, and Picts' houses; but these are generally unsatisfactory and lead to contradictory results.

Hugh Miller mentions bronze articles as being found along with rude implements of bone and flint, in shell-mounds, near Cromarty. Mr. George Petrie gives several instances of bronze, and even iron, having been found in apparent association with stone and bone, in Orkney, although he adds his own opinion, that the former are probably of later date. Mr. Rhind found bronze articles, along with shells, bones, and rude implements of stone and bone, in the chambered cairns of Kettleburn, in Caithness.

The result, therefore, hitherto has been to leave the age of these refuse heaps altogether uncertain. They might be of any age, from that of the Danish "Kjøkkenmöddings" to the historical or even the Christian period.

To add to the confusion of this period of British archæology, it appears that if there were ages of Stone, Bronze, and Iron in Britain, and Allophylian, or races different from the Indo-European family, who preceded the historical Kelts, the type of these races probably differed from those of the corresponding periods in Denmark. The earliest race of the Stone period in Scandinavia seem to have had small round heads like those of the Laplanders, and to have been succeeded in the Bronze period by a race whose skulls were extremely flat-sided and elongated. In this country it is held by Wilson and other authorities who maintain the existence of two pre-historic Allophylian races, that the long heads came first and the round heads second in succession.

This question of the type of race is alike difficult and important. It is difficult, for the type of a skull is not like the finding of a flint or bronze weapon, a definite fact. The skulls of a mixed and civilized race include a great variety of type, and although it is probable that primitive and savage races may retain more uniformity, still a wide margin must be allowed for accidental variation; and we must be quite sure that we have a considerable number of skulls of the same race under the same circumstances, all presenting the same marked type, before we can safely assume it as a foundation for classification, and a fact to guide further enquiry. It is worth any pains, however, to establish such a fact, if it be possible, for the determination of the cranial type of one of the early races, opens up questions of the highest interest. For instance, the question of round or long heads not only raises that of the priority or simultaneousness of the earliest waves of population in Britain and Scandinavia; but also of their connection with other primitive races still existing. Admitting the round and long-headed types in their superior forms to blend together in the more mixed and civilized races, it is still true that in their extreme and inferior form they characterize totally different sections of mankind. United with small brain and especially with small frontal capacity, large sinuses and prognatheus jaws, they indicate certainly an inferior, and probably a barbarous and unimprovable race. The extreme of the round-headed type is the Arctic Savage—the Laplander and Samoeide; the extreme of the elongated type is the Southern Savage—the Negro, Negrillo, and Australian. Did our primitive population come with the hippopotamus, whose bones are found in the Thames Valley, northwards; or with the reindeer and Siberian mammoth, southwards? This is a question which some day may be ripe for solution.

Again the question of type has a special interest from its bearings on that of progressive development. Is it or is it not a general rule that, speaking broadly and of long periods, the human race as we ascend in time, approximates to the quadrumana? The evidence thus far is conflicting; the Neanderthal skull giving us an answer in the affirmative, and the Engis skull one as distinctly in the negative. It is clear that facts are wanting to enable us to draw just conclusions, and that the class of facts is precisely that which is required to clear up the pre-historic period of British archæology, and connect it with that of the Continent.

I may state, therefore, the problem which I proposed to myself in commencing these explorations, in the following terms:

By a careful and scrupulously accurate examination of some of the middens or refuse-heaps of the North of Scotland, to ascertain their age and probable relations to those of Denmark.

From their contents to infer the condition of the people by whom they had been accumulated and specially to see whether the distinction of a Stone, Bronze, and Iron period could or could not be maintained.

If possible to discover graves and skeletons of the earliest race connected with these middens so as to ascertain their mode of sepulture, and obtain some idea of their type.

In these objects I was unexpectedly successful, and although I am far from saying that I have solved the problem, I believe I may say that the facts which I am about to record, and the collection which I am enabled to deposit in this National Museum of Scottish Antiquities, throw considerable light upon it, and advance it some steps towards solution.

It is right to add that I am personally responsible for the accuracy of every fact which I am about to state, having taken every sketch, section, and measurement on the spot, and seen myself the exact position of every relic of interest.

The County of Caithness is exceedingly rich in monuments of a pre-historic age. The rocky coasts and commanding heights are not more thickly studded with the strongholds of Scandinavian pirates and mediæval barons, than are the shores and straths with large conical mounds showing traces of concentric walls, which are in all probability like the one I examined, the ruins of burgs or circular towers. In addition there are numerous chambered cairns and Picts' houses, like that at Kettleburn described by Mr. Rhind, and barrows or sepulchral tumuli of various forms and dimensions. There are also many traces of hut circles and other pre-historic dwellings of a humbler class than the circular burg; and numerous shell-middens, or refuse-heaps of the food of the ancient inhabitants, are found in connection with their dwellings. Those remains are all of precisely the same character as in the adjoining Orkney Islands. In the neighbourhood of Keiss Castle, where I resided for part of the autumn, there are the following mounds within a range of about two miles, beginning from the south:

1. Two large mounds, popularly known as the "Birkle Hills," in the sandy links near the Westerburn.

2. A long "Burial mound," containing numerous stone kists and skeletons, about a mile and a half north of the former, where the links end, and the first houses of Keiss begin.

3. A large green mound, a little to the north of the harbour of Keiss, which I shall designate as the "Harbour mound," and immediately adjoining to it a smaller mound and some traces of ancient dwellings. These are about half a mile north of the Burial mound.

4. About a quarter of a mile inland from the "Harbour mound," close to the present churchyard, are two low, irregular, green mounds, one of which has been partly cut through by the road from Wick to Huna, disclosing a mass of shells. This I call the "Churchyard mound."

5. About three miles inland from Keiss, in the midst of an expanse of heather, is a small green spot with some grey stones scattered over it, which contains the remains of ancient dwellings. This I call the "Moorland mound."

There are many other mounds in this part of the country, but I confine myself to those which I have examined personally. My time being limited, and subject to many interruptions, I could not complete the exploration of all of those I have mentioned, so as to disclose thoroughly their structure and contents, and was obliged to confine myself to those which promised the most immediate results for the special object I had in view, which was not so much the elucidation of architectural structure, as the collection of facts bearing on the composition of the refuse heaps, and on the type and age of the race whose graves were unexpectedly disclosed while pursuing the former branch of research.

I begin with the "Burial mound," as the most important and interesting. At the point where the sandy links end, and the sand of the sea-shore changes into rock, a long, low,

OF CAITHNESS. 11

irregular mound of sand, overgrown with green turf, extends for about three hundred yards parallel to the beach on its natural terrace, which is here composed of a raised beach of sand and shingle. The mound has, probably, continued for four hundred or five hundred yards further north, over the space now occupied by cottages, gardens, and farm-yards, as kists and skeletons are said to have been found up to the point where the cliff of boulder clay rises near the harbour. In this case the mound has been nearly half a mile long.

Its shape is so far obliterated that it is not easy to assign its precise breadth and height, and, unless to an antiquarian eye, sharpened by the knowledge that kists had been found, the existence of a mound at all would escape notice. To this circumstance it is probably owing that the graves had in no instance been previously opened and the skeletons lay quite undisturbed. It is quite possible also that the mound may be composed principally of drift sand.

The maximum breadth may be taken roughly

at eighty to ninety yards, and the height at ten feet above the natural soil or raised beach, which is itself about ten feet above the highest level of the present high water mark.

The fact of this mound containing graves was disclosed by a road being cut through it about twenty years ago. Hearing of this, I made several cross sections, in search of kists, with the following results.

Kists were found in every instance with wonderful regularity at about fifteen feet apart, in the central line of the mound. They were all undisturbed and contained human skeletons, and were all of the same structure, consisting of walls of unhewn flag stones from the beach, with no floor, but covered with large flat stones. The kists generally lay north and south, or at a slight angle to the direction of the mound and seashore, which was north-east and south-west. The skeletons were all laid at full length, except one, in which the head and legs seem to have been partially crumpled up, but this may have arisen from subsequent displacement by pressure.

Fig. 3.

The skeletons lay in no particular direction, the heads being generally towards the south, but in some cases to the north. Nor were they laid in any particular position, most of them reclining on the right side, but one lying flat on its back, and others with their faces almost downwards. The bones were in various states of decomposition, according to local accidents giving more or less access to air and water. In two kists the skeletons had almost disappeared, or crumbled to pieces on being exposed to the air. In five instances they were nearly or quite perfect, but had lost much of their animal matter, and adhered strongly to the tongue.

The skeletons lay on a layer of clean sand, about six inches thick, laid on the natural soil, and above each kist was a small cairn or pile of stones from the beach, from one to three feet high, and above this, one to three feet of sand, covered with a fine grassy turf. In one instance the kists lay in a double tier, one over the other. The kists were generally filled with clean sea-sand, in which the body seemed to have been packed, or which had drifted in through the interstices of the roof, though others contained nothing but the skeleton.

There were no traces whatever of dwellings, of the action of fire, or of refuse heaps, in connection with the graves or burial mound ; a few of the kists only containing some shells, which may have been placed there as food for the deceased.

We may consider this burial mound, therefore, as a pure, unadulterated place of interment, which has never been disturbed, or used for any other purpose, and in which we have a series of probably sixty or seventy graves, taking the mound at three hundred yards in length, or of two hundred, if it extended, as there is every reason to believe, for half a mile. The number and regularity of the kists preclude the idea of a hurried interment of bodies slain in battle ; and some of the skeletons being of women, confirms the supposition that it was the regular burying-place of a surrounding population.

I proceed to describe the articles found in the kists with the human skeletons, which is the point of real importance in determining their age. In no instance was there a vestige of hair, integument, clothing, wooden coffin, urn, pottery, or, in fact, of anything whatever having been buried with the body, with the following exceptions.

In one kist the lower jaw of a dog was found. In two others were found stone weapons and implements, under the following circumstances. Disappointed at finding nothing to identify the age in any, of the first nine or ten kists opened, I considered that if any chief of superior rank were buried, it would probably be in the centre of the mound, and his grave would be the most likely place to discover relics. Accordingly, I had two trenches cut across the mound as nearly as possible at its centre, observing the rule which had hitherto been found to prevail, of an interval of fifteen feet between each grave. The northernmost trench disclosed the kist No. 7, in which lay the skeleton of a man much taller than any of the others previously opened, being nearly six feet in height, while those previously found did not exceed five feet to five feet four inches; and by his side, in

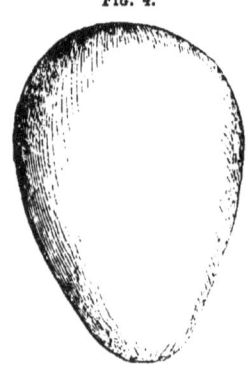

Fig. 4.

Stone Hammer or Celt from Kist No. 7.—⅓ nat. size.

the clean sea-sand which filled the kist, was a heart-shaped stone hammer or celt (fig. 4), with some limpet shells. It is a naturally rolled stone from the beach of sandstone, 5 inches long, 3¾ inches broad, and about an inch thick, and bears evident marks of having been used at the smaller end.

The other trench hit upon the corner of a circular wall which we at first took for the wall of a small burg or round tower, but on examination it proved to be an inclosing wall, eighteen feet in inner diameter, about two and a half feet high, and nine inches to one foot thick, of a cairn of stones, which as we approached the centre became large, and were disposed with some care. On removing the cairn was disclosed a stone

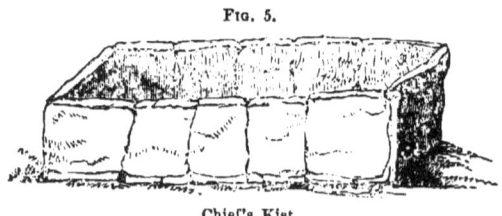

Fig. 5.

Chief's Kist.

kist of large dimensions (fig. 5), built and roofed over with massive flat stones, shown in the accompanying sketch and section (figs. 6, 7).

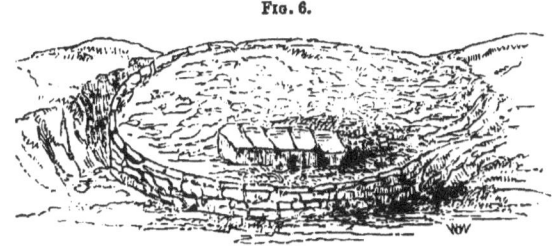

Fig. 6.

Chief's Kist and Cairn.

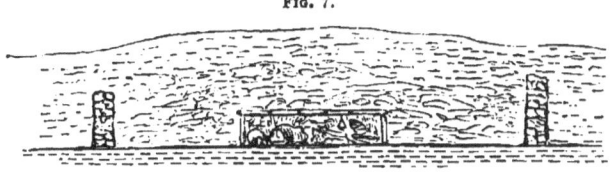

Fig. 7.

Section of Chief's Kist and Cairn.

The dimensions of the kist were: length, 6 feet 7 inches; width at head, 1 foot 10 inches; width at foot, 1 foot 9 inches; depth, 1 foot 10 inches.

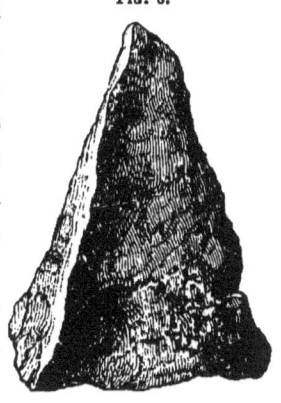

Fig. 8.

It contained the skeleton of a tall man of very massive proportions. He lay with his head to the south, in the usual attitude, on his right side; and in the clean sand by his side, about where the left hand reached to, were a series of twelve stone weapons, marked "Kist No. 8," which may be safely said to be among the very rudest ever used by man.

They comprise,—one which may have been a battle-axe, two which may have been spear-heads, one arrow-head, seven knives or

Stone Battle-axe. Chief's Kist.
¼ nat. size.

cutting instruments, and one which seems to be the fragment of a broken celt or hammer.

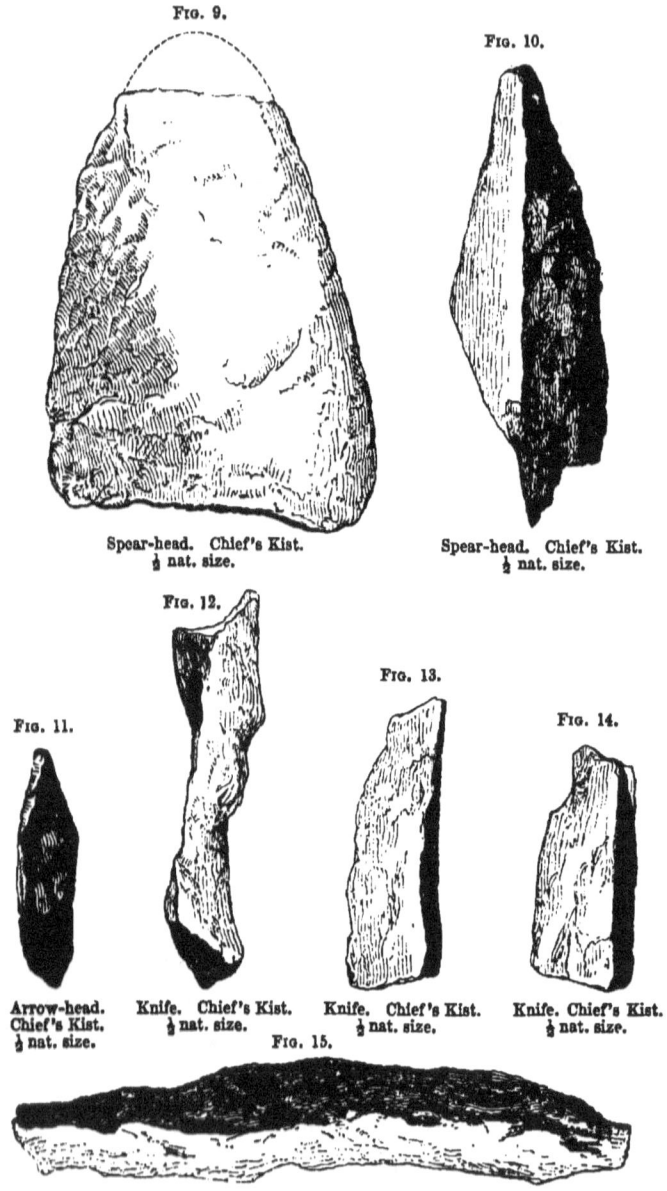

Fig. 9.
Spear-head. Chief's Kist. ½ nat. size.

Fig. 10.
Spear-head. Chief's Kist. ½ nat. size.

Fig. 11.
Arrow-head. Chief's Kist. ½ nat. size.

Fig. 12.
Knife. Chief's Kist. ½ nat. size.

Fig. 13.
Knife. Chief's Kist. ½ nat. size.

Fig. 14.
Knife. Chief's Kist. ½ nat. size.

Fig. 15.
Knife. Chief's Kist. ½ nat. size.

Fig. 16.
Knife or Scraper. Chief's Kist.
½ nat. size.

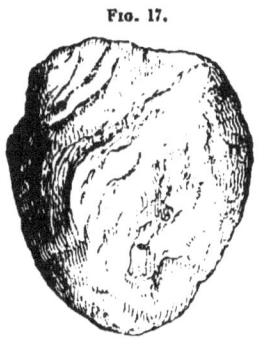
Fig. 17.
Knife or Scraper. Chief's Kist.
½ nat. size.

In addition to these, there were laid under the head, or close to it, an oval sandstone disc (fig. 18) and knife, and a

Fig. 18.
Sandstone Disc. Chief's Kist. ¼ nat. size.

smooth oval beach stone, apparently intended for a hammer. This makes in all fifteen stone weapons or implements found in the chief's kist.

There were further found among the stones in the cairn covering the chief's kist, five stone articles, viz.—

1. A sandstone block, 13 inches in diameter, with two circular holes about 2 inches deep, on opposite sides, but not pierced through. (See pl. vii., fig. 9.)

2. A thin plate, 18 inches by 14, rudely chipped to an oval or circular form.

3. A similar round plate, about 7 inches by 6.

4. A broken wrought circular stone, with a circular hole in the centre, not pierced through.

5. A small granite stone from the beach, apparently used as a hammer, 2½ inches by 1¾.

Several other stones were found, of very regular oval form, which may have been celts or hammers, but natural stones of this description are so common on the beach that I made a rule of rejecting everything which did not bear unequivocal marks of having been wrought or used by man.

Since I left Keiss another kist has been opened in this mound containing, with a skeleton which crumbled to pieces, another armoury of similar weapons which by the kindness of Mr. Anderson, of Wick, who is well known for his

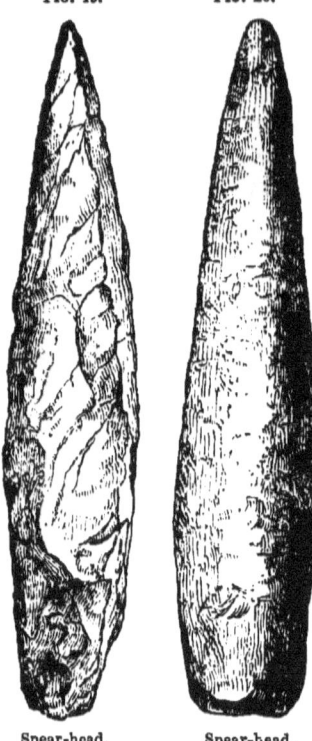

Fig. 19. Fig. 20.
Spear-head. Spear-head.
Kist No. 9. Kist No. 9.

Fig. 21. Fig. 22.
Arrow-head. Arrow-head.
Kist No. 9. Kist No. 9.

knowledge of the geology and antiquities of Caithness, are presented along with mine to the museum. They are labelled "Kist No. 9," and consist of two small spear-heads of stone, roughly ground or scraped to shape, but better wrought than any in Kist No. 8; two stone arrow-heads very rudely chipped; a piece of quartz rudely chipped to a form which may have been used as a chisel; a small deer's-horn hollowed out apparently to serve as a handle; an oblong stone hammer or pestle worn at both ends (figs. 19-24).

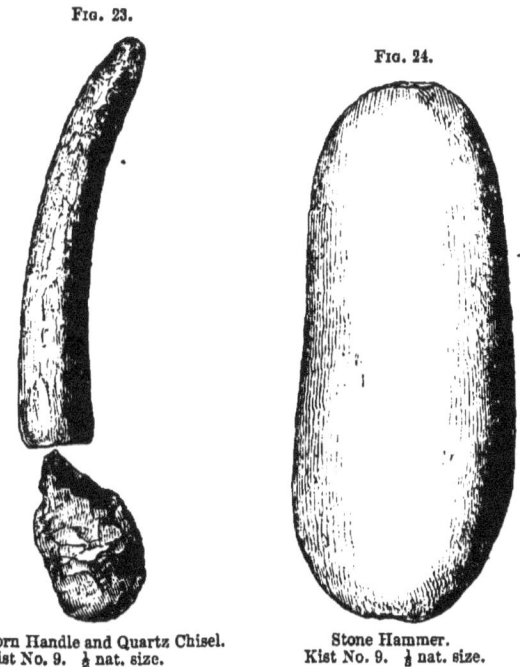

Fig. 23.

Fig. 24.

Deer's-horn Handle and Quartz Chisel.
Kist No. 9. ½ nat. size.

Stone Hammer.
Kist No. 9. ½ nat. size.

I proceed now to the other mounds, and begin with the Churchyard mound, as affording the simplest state of facts, and the closest analogy to the Danish Kjökkenmöddings.

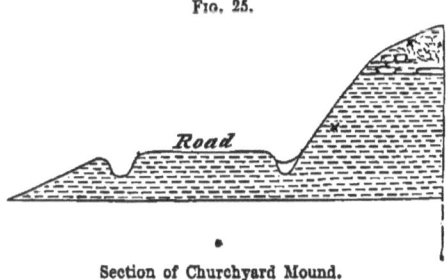

Fig. 25.

Section of Churchyard Mound.

In this case, as shown in the accompanying section (fig. 25), a great mass of shells, at least five feet deep, and covering an area of several hundred square yards, rests on the natural soil, and is itself covered by the foundation of a massive building, which in its turn has all but disappeared, and been converted into a low and shapeless green mound, affording excellent pasture.

I am inclined to think that the old building may have been a burg, or circular tower, like that presently to be described, on the shore; but even the ruins have almost disappeared, having doubtless been used as a quarry for building adjoining houses and stone walls; and nothing remains but the massive pavement or floor of large flat stones, three to four inches thick, and just enough of structure in one place to show that the principle of overlapping stones was used as a substitute for the arch.

However, the important fact remains, that this foundation is super-imposed on the shell-mound as clearly as any secondary is on a primary formation in geology; and that the refuse heap cannot have accumulated about the building, but must have existed before it.

This heap is composed mainly of periwinkle shells, differing in this respect from the others nearer the shore, in which limpets predominate. There are, however, mixed with it several limpet shells, and a few of the other species found on the shore, and a considerable number of animal bones and teeth, almost all of which are chipped up into small fragments.

The relics found in this heap, principally towards the middle and lower strata, consist of chipped flints, and very rude stone and bone implements and pottery. There are specially two bone arrow-heads, and about eighteen skewers or pins of fragments of bone and horn, worked roughly to a point, which may be appealed to confidently as a proof of the absence of metals, and extreme rudeness of the race by which they were used. They are, in fact, the *ne plus ultra* of rudeness in bone, as the weapons found in the kist are of a like rudeness in implements of stone (figs. 26-31).

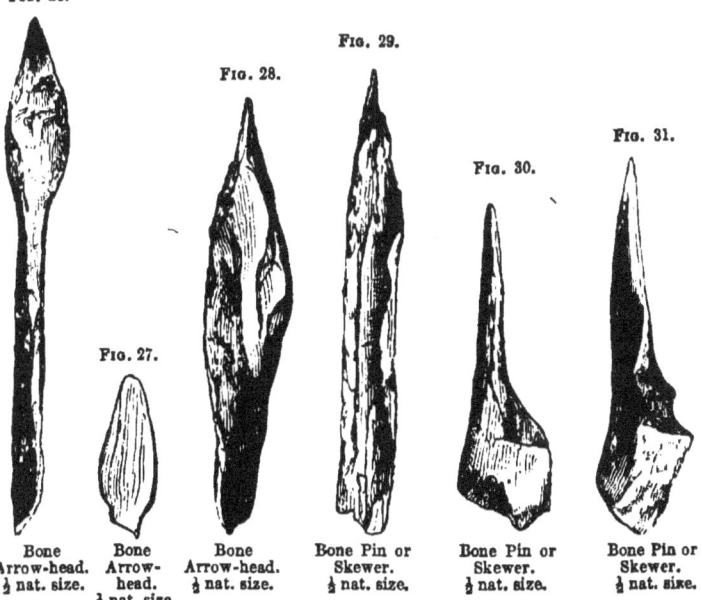

Fig. 26. Bone Arrow-head. ½ nat. size.
Fig. 27. Bone Arrow-head. ½ nat. size.
Fig. 28. Bone Arrow-head. ½ nat. size.
Fig. 29. Bone Pin or Skewer. ½ nat. size.
Fig. 30. Bone Pin or Skewer. ½ nat. size.
Fig. 31. Bone Pin or Skewer. ½ nat. size.

In the centre of the mass, at the point marked × in the section, was found a human tooth, with a small portion of the jaw, which is important in connection with a similar discovery in another mound. Wood ashes and charcoal were common in this mound, and the shells and bones appeared to have been generally subjected to the action of fire.

The animal bones were less abundant, and more generally chipped into small pieces than those found in the other mounds. It seemed as if four-fifths of the food of the people by whom this most ancient midden had been accumulated, had consisted of periwinkles, and as if animal bones had been a delicacy, from which every particle of marrow was extracted by breaking them up. The extreme rarity of fish-bones in this and the other middens is a curious feature in a locality where fish are so abundant.

The only stone implements were oval beach stones which had been used as hammers or pestles, a rude stone mortar, and several round pebbles or slingstones about the size of an apple, which had evidently been selected from the beach. These natural slingstones and hammers were the most common objects in this and all the other mounds.

The pottery was all in small fragments of the rudest description, and not distinguishable from the specimens I have seen of hand-made unburnt pottery from the Danish Kjökkenmöddings.

Although chipped flints were abundant, and several of the splinters might have been used as small knives or arrow-heads, none of them showed such clear traces of definite design as to justify their being called tools or weapons. In fact, the whole series of relics from this midden show a *minimum* of adaptive ingenuity, with the exception of one whorl, which I believe came from it (though not having found this myself, I cannot speak with absolute confidence), which may be taken to indicate a knowledge of spinning.

Fig. 32.

Harbour Mound.

The next mound I shall describe is the Harbour mound, which afforded the greatest number of relics, and showed most clearly the architectural structure of these ancient

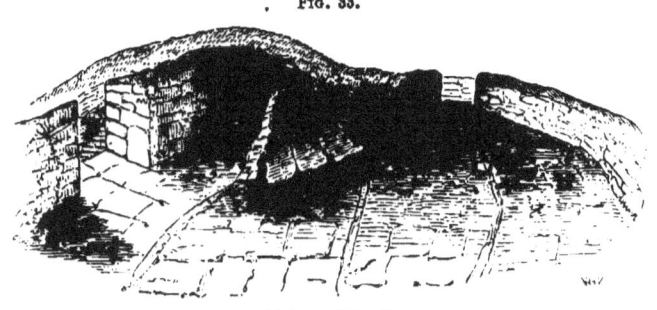

Fig. 33.

Harbour Mound.

dwellings. At first sight it consisted of a very irregular grassy mound, with some loose stones lying about, and showing faint traces of a low outer circular wall or rampart. On excavating, a great mass of cyclopean building and shell-midden was disclosed, with floors or pavements at different levels, which will be best explained by the accompanying sketches, ground plan, and sections (figs. 32-36).

It is clear that this building had been of the class of burg or circular tower, common in Caithness and Orkney. I doubt, however, whether it ever had the bee-hive shape, as no sign of convergence appears in any of the circular walls, one of which remained standing in parts to the height of twelve feet. It seems

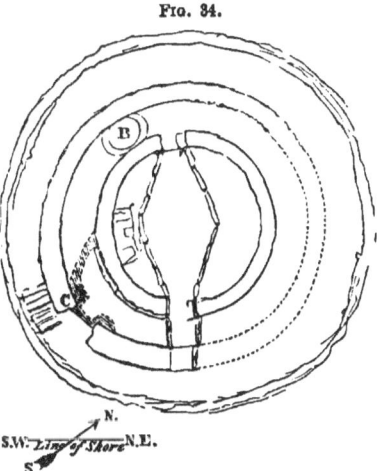

Fig. 34.

Harbour Mound. Ground Plan.

DIMENSIONS: feet.
Diameter of inner circle, about 24
Thickness of inner wall...................... 2
Passage between inner and second wall... 3
Thickness of second wall 4
Space between second and outer wall,—
  variable .... 4 to 15
Thickness of outer wall...................... 1½ to 2

rather as if the passages only between the circular walls had been covered in, and used as dwellings in bad weather or winter, the inner circle, which is twenty-four feet in diameter, remaining open.

The whole upper part of the building, however, has fallen in, and a great part of it, including nearly all the circular walls on the northern side, removed for building purposes. No vestige of timber was found, though there was abundance of wood charcoal in the lower strata, apparently of a small scrubby underwood of birch and hazel.

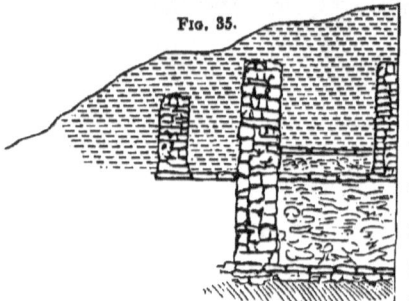

Fig. 35.
Harbour Mound. First Section at C.

The remarkable fact in this mound is, that it indicated successive occupation, and adaptation of the older parts of the building by newer inhabitants. The primitive part of the structure seemed to be the second or middle circular wall, which was by far the most massively built, and went down to a lower pavement of large flags, resting on a layer of flat beach stones, laid on the natural rock. The space for five feet above this level was filled up with a midden, or accumulation of shells, bones, ashes, etc. Then came a second pavement of large flag-stones, on a level with which are the foundations of the two other—or inner and outer circular walls. Above this was another midden, one-and-a-half feet deep, and then an upper pavement, forming the

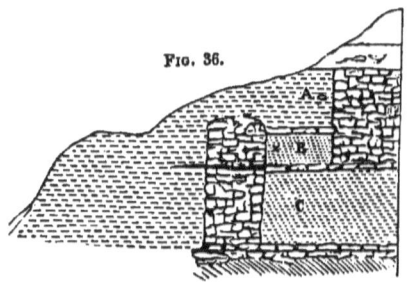

Fig. 36.
Harbour Mound. Second Section at B.

floor of the inner circle. This, again, was covered by a midden of its own, mixed with a mass of stones and rubbish which had fallen in and choked up the building. There were thus three distinct middens, separated by superimposed pavements, which, without expressing any theory, and simply as a convenient mode of representing the facts, I may call the primary, secondary, and tertiary middens.

Outside the walls, these middens were of course less distinct, there being no pavements to separate them; but it was evident that as the refuse had accumulated at each stage on the floors inside, it had accumulated still more rapidly on the outside at certain spots where it had been commonly thrown out; and thus the same distinction of a primary, secondary, and tertiary midden must approximately apply nearly to the same levels of the outside strata.

In addition to the evidence from superposition of pavements, there is clear proof of successive occupation, from other sources. The doorways of the inner and second circular walls do not correspond. The former has two entrances, as shown on the ground-plan, nearly opposite to each other, or east and west. The other has one very massive doorway

FIG. 37.

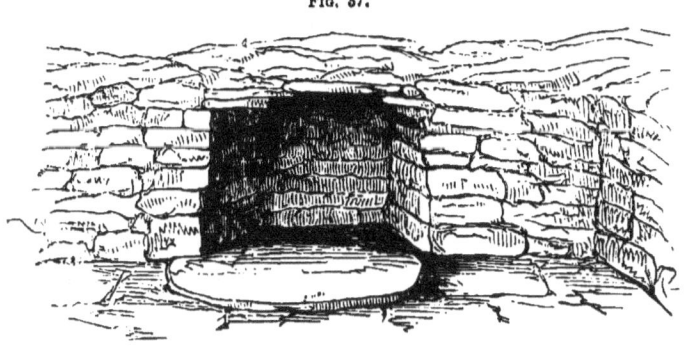

only, to the south-west. On coming up to this doorway in exploring the passage, between the two circular walls, it presented the appearance of a fire-place and chimney, rudely constructed with loose rubbly stones, overlapping one another, as shown in the accompanying sketch (fig. 37).

On removing these, the solid massive doorway of the

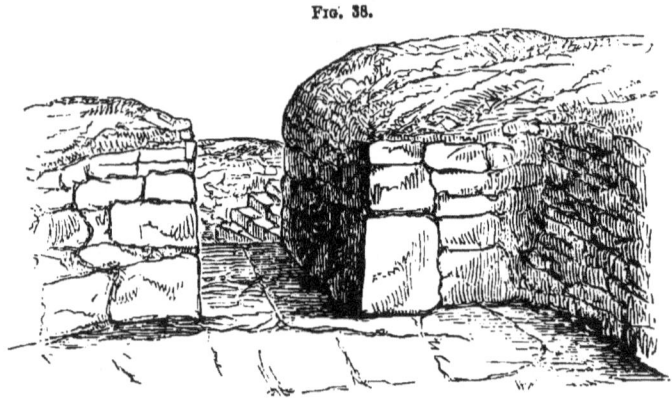

FIG. 38.

second wall appeared, which had obviously been converted from the entrance of a strong fort into a chimney (fig. 38).

Just outside this doorway was a massive stone staircase of eleven steps, leading down to the level of the second pavement.

I am particular in stating these facts, as they have an important bearing on this other fact, that the class of relics found in the upper and lower middens were essentially distinct. Among the various relics from this and the other mounds, there is no exception to the rule, that the rude forms of bone and pottery are exclusively confined to the two lower middens, while the few instances of metallic objects, finer pottery, and well-wrought bone implements are as exclusively confined to the upper one. The same rule applies generally to the stone implements, but these are more intermixed, as might be expected of heavy objects where so much of the original building has fallen in, or been quarried and disturbed.

The skulls, and animal teeth and bones, were of the same character throughout, and very abundant, so that many cart loads might be taken, in addition to what had been already taken—as I was told—to manure the land. The larger bones had generally been broken to extract the marrow; but not into such small fragments as in the Churchyard mound, though the same rule seemed to apply here to some extent, that the bones were broken into smaller pieces in the lower strata. The large deers' horns especially seemed to be most abundant towards the top. Several of them bear marks of sawing or cutting, so clean that they must have been made by better instruments, either of metal or sharp flint, than any of those found in the kists or middens. The shells

FIG. 39.

are principally limpet, a mass of which, cemented by oxide of iron, is preserved as a specimen (fig. 39).

Wood charcoal and ashes were common in the lower middens, while higher up the ashes seemed to be of peat.

The relics found in this mound consisted of—1. Rude stone implements, chipped flints, rude implements of bone and horn, and coarse, hand-made pottery, which correspond in character with those found in the Churchyard middens and burial mound. 2. A bronze implement resembling a sugar tongs (fig. 40), and an iron object, apparently the two blades of a pair of scissors rusted together, which were found close together in the upper midden, at or near the spot marked A in the section with some thinner and finer pottery. The iron is probably comparatively recent, and a relic of the last occupants of the dwellings by whom the chimney and fireplace were constructed.

Fig. 40.

Bronze tongs or tweezers. ½ nat. size.

In the secondary midden, B, at the spot marked ×, in the midst of a mass of limpet shells, and broken jaws, teeth, and bones of animals, I found the fragment of a human lower jaw. It is that of a child about six years of age, the permanent teeth being formed, but not having yet displaced the milk teeth. No trace of any other human bone was found with it, and coupling it with the fact of another isolated fragment of human jaw having been found in another midden, both under circumstances precisely similar to those of the deer, pigs, and oxen by which they were surrounded, it raises a strong presumption that these aboriginal savages were occasionally cannibals.

The fact is the more remarkable, as the extensive researches in the Danish Kjökkenmöddings have failed to discover any trace of human bones, whence Lyell infers, in his "Antiquity of Man," that the primeval Danes were not cannibals.

I may add, in confirmation of the fact of occasional cannibalism, that fragmentary human remains have been found in several other refuse heaps in Caithness, and that Professor Owen, whose attention has been specially directed to the

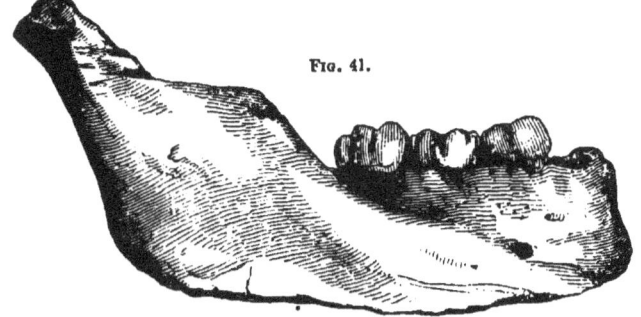

Fig. 41.

Child's Jaw from Midden. nat. size.

subject, considers that the child's jaw above referred to, has been splintered open precisely in the manner in which ani-

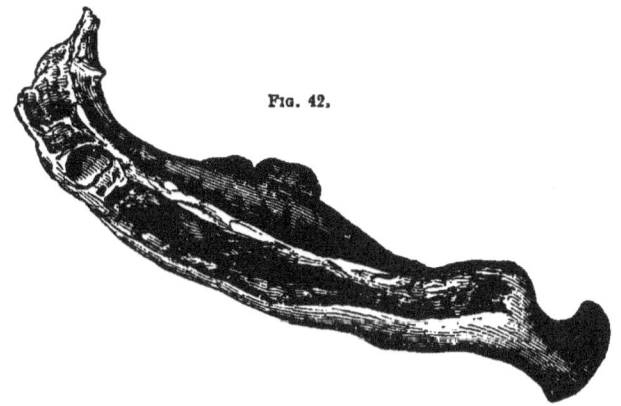

Fig. 42.

Child's Jaw, showing splintering to extract marrow.

mal jaws are frequently opened by human agency to extract the juices of the dentary canal, and not in the way in which a dog or wolf would have gnawed the bone.

The question of cannibalism is, however, one of little scientific interest, as there are historical notices of such a practice reputed to prevail among the barbarous tribes of Caledonia as late as the time of St. Jerome, and human flesh may have been eaten under the pressure of famine by races who were not habitual cannibals. I notice it principally as affording a point of contrast to the Danish Kjökkenmöddings.

The next mounds to be described are the Birkle Hills.

These are two mounds situated on the Wester links, large enough to be taken—as their name implies—for small natural hills, as shown by the accompanying sketch (fig. 43). They stand amidst the hillocks of blown sand, about two hundred

Fig. 43.

Birkle Hills.

yards from the sea-shore, on the raised beach of sand and flat shingle stones, which can here be traced distinctly for some distance. The larger mound is roughly conical, about forty feet high, and one hundred and twenty yards in circumference at the base. The lower mound commences about one hundred yards north-east of the other, and is a long, irregular mound, which may be taken roughly at thirty feet high, one hundred yards long, and thirty yards wide. The surface of both mounds is of sand, covered with small stones from the adjacent raised beach, and, in the case of the smaller mound especially, with a vast number of limpet and periwinkle shells, and animal teeth and bones. Traces of small cairns of massive stones remain on the summits of both mounds and round their base, but these seem all to have been opened, and disclosed no structure or relics. At the base of the smaller mound, on the side next the sea, was a stone kist, exactly like those of the Burial mound, the head stone of which just projected above the sand. It had been opened—I believe a few years ago, by a medical man now in India—but the skeleton, with the exception of the skull, which was wanting, had been replaced in the kist. The remains of three or four other kists of similar construction lay scattered about the base of the small mound; and on the west side of the large mound one was found containing some small fragments of human bones, with some skulls and portions of animal bones, but these latter may have fallen into the kist from the surrounding soil. One of these kists has since been found to contain six stone weapons of the same rude type as those of the Burial mound, which, by the kindness of Mr. Anderson, I am enabled to add to this collection. One is an extremely rude spear-head; another apparently a small curved spear-head made from the conchoidal fracture of a piece of sandstone from the beach; two very rude sandstone knives or scrapers like those from Kist No. 8; a small quartz chisel like that from No. 9; and a stone hammer or pestle somewhat more regularly formed than those of Nos. 8 & 9 and abraded into a circular spot at each end (figs. 44-48).

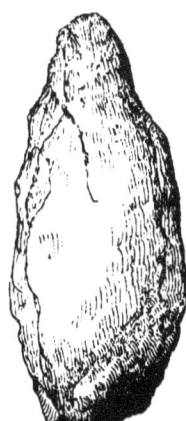

Fig. 44.
Spear-head.
Birkle Hill Kist.
½ nat. size.

Fig. 45. 
Spear-head.
Birkle Hill Kist.
½ nat. size.

The most important point about these kists is, that they serve to connect the mounds on the links with the Burial mound, the age of which is defined by the implements found in the chief's kist. The kists are of precisely the same size and construction, except that some of them at the Birkle

Hills seem to have had two memorial pillars or small standing stones, about three feet in height, one on each side of the head-stone of the kist.

As regards the structure of these mounds, I had no time to investigate it thoroughly. The larger mound shows traces of Cyclopean

Fig. 47.

Fig. 46.

Fig. 48.

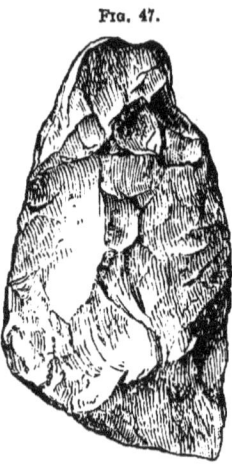

Sandstone Knife.
Birkle Hill Kist.
½ nat. size.

Quartz Chisel.
Birkle Hill Kist.

Stone Hammer.
Birkle Hill Kist.
½ nat. size.

architecture, and I am disposed to think it is of the same class as the other large conical mounds of Caithness, viz., consisting of concentric circular walls with cells or chambers in the interspaces between the walls. I am somewhat doubtful, however, of its having been a fort or dwelling, from the circumstance that, with the exception of a few shells and bones scattered sparingly over the surface, no trace of any midden or refuse heap was seen.

The smaller mound, on the other hand, was completely covered with shells, teeth, and bones; and, in excavating, considerable masses of midden were disclosed. Everywhere, also, the action of fire was apparent, and several of the cairns seemed to be the remains of small circular ovens or fire-places which had been used for roasting the animals whose bones lay around them.

The only instance of complete structure disclosed was at the top of the small mound, as shown by the accompanying plan and section (figs. 49, 50).

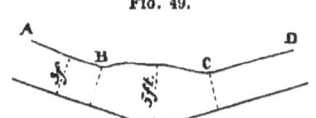

Birkle Hill. Small Mound. Ground Plan.

A very massive stone closed the entrance on the east side next the sea. From this a passage, enclosed on each side by upright flagstones, about two feet long by one and a half deep, descended by a very gentle decline for six feet. It then became horizontal for about eight feet, widening out from three to five feet, and taking a turn from nearly north-west to west, in which direction a similar ascending passage emerged on the west side of the mound.

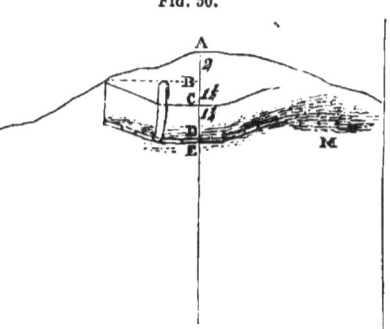

Birkle Hill. Small Mound. Section.

Between the upright flags were placed, in several instances, oblong stones about three feet high, similar to the memorial stones of the kists. The stones were all unhewn, and must have been brought from the beach from a distance of at least two miles. They were built with some care, stones being placed in some cases to fill interstices and break joint. There was no trace of a roof, but the pavement was carefully fitted.

Refuse of shells, bone, animal matter, and charcoal had accumulated on this floor to the depth of about nine inches, and when the pavement was taken up it showed a few inches of similar refuse below on which the flags had been laid.

The refuse matter and pavement all showed signs of fire, which became more intense in the central chamber where the bones were all charred and many of the stones split by heat.

The west end of the passage was not closed, but was partially ruined, and outside of it was a considerable midden of the usual shells and bones.

The relics found were:—1. In the lower midden, two small whorls of stone and one of bone; the latter (fig.51) is worth noticing. It is made of the ball of a femur, and from its lightness and hemispherical form seems to negative the idea that it could ever have been used for the purpose of spinning. Some pieces of flint which have been artificially chipped. A broken sandstone block, six inches by four, resembling a ship's block, having a deep groove running round it, with a notch at one end for the purpose of attachment; I have seen a stone exactly similar, though smaller, in the collection of Mr. George Petrie, which was found at Grain, near Kirkwall, in Orkney, in cutting a road near the site of a ruined Pict's house. Such grooved stones have also been found in Denmark, where they are supposed to have been sinkers for fishing lines or nets. I feel some doubt whether such was the object in the present case, as the extreme rarity of fish bones in all the middens described, makes it improbable that they were accumulated by a race of fishermen. The notch at the lower end also seems to have been intended for inserting a handle to be secured by lashing a thong round it in the line of the groove. It is singular that

Fig. 51.

Bone Whorl.
½ nat. size.

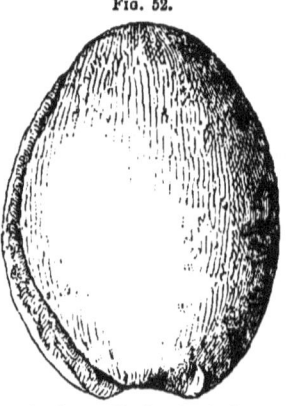

Fig. 52.

Sandstone Block.—½ nat. size.

a similar grooved block is figured among the objects from the Lake-habitations of Italy, in the translation of Gastaldi's work published by the Anthropological Society, pl. 1, fig. 2. A stone hammer or oval beach stone, showing signs of pounding at the end. 2. In the upper strata of the outside midden were found a bone skewer and particularly well-

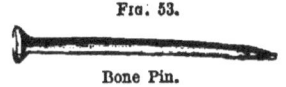

Bone Pin.

fashioned bone pin (fig. 53) with a regular head, and apparently fashioned after one in metal; being the only instance of a skilfully wrought bone relic among these remains. Above these, in the clean sand about two feet below the surface of the mound, was found a large iron nail, much corroded, and some small fragments of rusted iron. On the surface of the mound were found, amidst the numerous shells and bones and ordinary beach stones, some flint pebbles and splinters of flint, two small pieces of chalk much weatherworn, part of a belemmite, bits of rock crystal, and large iron pyrites, one or two rusty nails, apparently recent, one of them sticking in a piece of wood; some fragments of light vegetable matter, probably highly dried peat; and a large lump, not waterworn, of black magnetic iron ore, with one or two small pieces of the same slightly fused.

There were, however, no traces of slag or of iron furnaces; and what is singular, considering the extent and varied nature of the débris exposed and turned over, not a trace was found of pottery. In fact the small proportion of relics found in these as compared with the other mounds leads to the supposition that they may not have been regular dwellings, but rather places of worship or sacrifice, when the neighbouring tribes met to regale themselves with rude banquets. Further excavations, however, would be necessary to disclose the structure of these mounds, as to which, all that can be said with any certainty is that they are of the same period as the Burial mound and the lower strata of the other mounds, as is clearly proved by the construction and contents of the kists.

The remaining or Moorland mound is of a different character, and falls rather within the class of pre-historic dwellings described by the Rev. Mr. Joass, in Mr. Roberts's paper. The dwelling explored, however, is not circular, but nearly square, with an entrance passage as shown by the subjoined sketch and plan (figs. 54–56).

The walls are made of large flags set on edge; there was no trace of any roof, but the floor was paved with flat stones, over which were a few inches to a foot of shells, bones, and ashes. The shells were principally periwinkles, though the distance from the shore was about three miles, and there were several large fish bones. The other bones were principally of deer, pigs, and birds. Along the wall on each side of the principal room was a row of square boulder stones, forming a bench or bed. The inner end was divided by two large upright flagstones into three compartments. The fireplace had been on the stone floor near the passage or doorway.

The relics found on clearing out the floor of this dwelling were,—

Some fragments of pottery, apparently wheel-made, and newer than that of the other mounds, one of the pieces having a coarse blue glaze.

A sandstone hammer or oval beach stone, used at the end.

Two small stone whorls.

Several smooth round pebbles from the beach, which I take to be slingstones.

A piece of porphyry, polished on one side.

From the nature of the pottery, I do not consider this

Moorland Mound.

dwelling or cluster of dwellings in the middle of the

Moorland Mound.

moor as of the same antiquity as the mounds near the

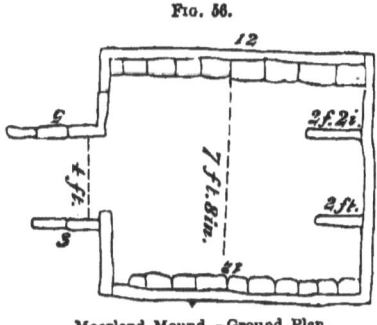

Moorland Mound.—Ground Plan.

shore, with which there is no evidence to connect them.

Having now completed the description of these mounds, I proceed to state the leading results.

ANTIQUITY.—I have no hesitation in assigning the burial mound, kists, and lower strata of the middens, to the early Stone period.

In using this term I do not mean to prejudge the question of absolute antiquity, for it may well be that an aboriginal tribe of savages have lingered on little changed in a remote corner of Britain, to a comparatively recent period. What I think certain is that these people were too rude to have known anything of the arts or metals current among the people of the later Stone or Bronze periods of the Continent and Britain; or to have superseded any earlier and less civilized races of prior aborigines. The evidence for this conclusion rests mainly on the weapons buried with the dead.

Those who have seen the admirable Museum of Northern Antiquities at Copenhagen must be aware that its whole classification rests on the axiom that greater rudeness implies greater antiquity. It is as difficult to believe that the Enfield rifle preceded the cross-bow, as that the beautifully-fashioned stone battle axes and flint arrow-heads of the later Stone period, preceded the rudely chipped celts and mauls of the Kjökkenmöddings. Now, tried by this test, the weapons and tools of the Caithness kists and lower middens are ruder and show less adaptive ingenuity than those of the Kjökkenmöddings, or even than those of Abbeville and Les Eyzies. The supposition has been started that they may have been merely models or "dummies," representing more perfect weapons, too valuable to be consigned to the grave. But this is contrary to all experience, which proves that when the idea of a future state was once entertained by a primitive people, no sacrifice was thought too costly to accompany the honoured dead. Nine-tenths of the richest contents of our museums come from tombs where they were deposited by affectionate reverence for the dead; and the Museum of Copenhagen has abundant instances to show that if, in a later age, models were deposited, they were always, although of miniature size, carefully fashioned; and that such an idea as that of depositing in the tomb of a great chief a rude fragment of sandstone, to do duty for a finely-finished spear-head of agate or bronze, was wholly unknown.

In fact, the articles deposited were the property of the deceased, and were buried with him precisely because they were valued. Moreover, in this case many of the weapons show traces of having been actually used; the points of the spear-heads are broken or blunted; the ends of the hammers are abraded; and to complete the link of evidence, spear and arrow-heads, hammers, and a deer-horn handle, of precisely similar patterns have been found in the middens.

The presence of such weapons in the kists affords, however, very different evidence from that furnished by finding similar remains in the middens. In the latter case it may be argued that if rude forms are found they may have been used concurrently with more perfect implements, the remains of which are wanting simply because they were too valuable to be thrown aside. Or it may be said that the rude remains are those of poor peasants, who may have lived at the same period as the chiefs, whose finer weapons are found in costly tombs.

But neither of these arguments can apply to a case like the present, where a series of weapons of the rudest possible material and construction, are found in the kist of a chief upon whose interment evidently great labour had been expended.

Admitting the weapons to be genuine, the argument for great relative antiquity becomes very cogent. Stone implements, like hammers or querns, might be used down to a late period, and buried with the dead as part of their household furniture, and finely-finished stone weapons might be placed in a kist of the Bronze or Iron period from some superstitious notion that they were elf-arrows or thunderbolts. But an armoury of the most rude and primitive possible forms of spear- and arrow-heads, knives, and hatchets, could hardly have been used by a people who had known, even by tradition, I will not say the use of metals, but even the more advanced forms of stone and bone which are so commonly found throughout Scotland, and in this very district.

To appreciate the full force of this argument it is necessary to inspect the articles referred to, as no drawings can give an adequate idea of their extreme rudeness. A reference, however, to the figures in the text, and to the plates at the end, may serve to give some conception of the primitive and archaic style of the weapons and tools of these Caithness aborigines, which contrasts so strikingly with that of the beautifully fashioned implements of polished stone and bronze of a later period, found in the same district.

It is to be observed that the stone weapons and tools are all of the native sandstone or common beach stones of the district. They are for the most part rounded or fractured by nature, or by a single blow, with the least possible adaptation by rough chipping. The hammers or celts are almost all natural stones from the beach.

The few which have been more carefully wrought into shape have been scraped or roughly ground, and are never polished. There is no instance of a hole in which to insert a handle, or even of a groove to facilitate attachment, except in the single case of one sandstone block which was not found in a kist or lower midden; and it may even be doubted whether some of the larger weapons and stone hammers were not simply held in the hand. In the two or three instances in which one end of the weapon was clearly inserted in a socket or haft, nothing can be ruder than the workmanship. In no instance is there the slightest trace of ornament even on the handles of bone and horn, which are so elaborately carved by the cave-dwellers of Les Eyzies. The same remark applies to the pottery; the rude specimens of which from the lower middens appear precisely similar to those of the Danish Kjökkenmöddings. To suppose, as some have done, that these relics may be as recent as the Christian era, is to cut away from under our feet all possible ground for archæological classification. It is undoubted that the Romans found Caledonia inhabited by races acquainted with iron, and possessing sufficient civilization and capacity for military and political organization, to oppose a formidable resistance to the legions of Agricola. What likelihood is there, that a people worse armed than the savages of the Andamans could have lived in the open defenceless plains of Caithness in contact with such races?

Again, if a people little advanced beyond the Stone period of Abbeville lived in Caithness and Orkney down to the Christian period, where can we intercalate the people to whom belong the innumerable cairns, bowl barrows, and other sepulchral and monumental remains of those two counties, which show evident signs of greatly advanced culture? These latter people were Pagans, for they burned their dead in the later barrows, and in the earlier ones buried them in a contracted posture in megalithic kists, under cairns or mounds, which may truly be called stupendous, and, having regard to their means may vie with the Pyramids. They reared temples, like the Stones of Stenness, which imply considerable population, and civilization up to the point where priests could wield the labour of masses by appealing to religious ideas. If the limpet-eating savages, with their rude sandstone knives, lived in these regions until the Christian era, the classification of the Copenhagen Museum must be inverted, and the sepulchral urns and finished ornaments of the Bronze period assigned to an earlier date than the rude implements of the Kjökkenmöddings.

I by no means contend for a high geological antiquity for these remains. On the contrary, the position of the mounds on the terrace of the present beach, which is itself a raised beach of the last slight elevation of ten or twelve feet, affords a presumption against great antiquity; and the existence of whorls may, as I shall hereafter point out, possibly indicate a knowledge of spinning, which, notwithstanding the rudeness of their weapons and cutting implements would place them at a higher level than the men of the Kjökkenmöddings.

But I think the evidence establishes that, whatever may be the period at which they lived, they must have been the earliest or aboriginal race, and prior to the people who at some later period, but antecedent to the Christian era, raised in these same regions so many remarkable monuments, and left so many relics in their tombs in the form of finely-wrought stone, bronze, sepulchral urns, and ornamented pottery.

I have heard but one objection raised to this conclusion. Some antiquarians hold that the burial in extended kists of necessity implies Christian influences and a recent period.

I believe this to be a complete fallacy. Some highly artificial modes of interment, like mummyfying or burning, may prove the continuance of certain religious ideas and lead us to infer identity of race and period; though even this is not always certain as there are savage races, like the Australians, who practise various modes of sepulture indiscriminately. But a method of interment can prove little, which is so obvious and simple as that of extended sepulture; or, in other words, inclosing the body, as it lies in its natural attitude on the ground, in a rude kist of flat beach stones set on edge, and covering it with a little grave mound of sand and stones. Indeed, so far as the matter can be reasoned out, it seems almost certain that such a simple mode of sepulture must have preceded the more ambitious attempts of a more advanced period to erect massive monuments. A large cairn or mound implies a megalithic and contracted kist, to support the weight; and a contracted kist necessitates contracted sepulture. Moreover, much may have depended on the nature of the material, and what is true where nothing but large schistose blocks were available, may not be true where, as in Orkney and Caithness, flags of moderate size and regularly squared by Nature, are the readiest material.

It is admitted that extended sepulture superseded cremation, as Christianity superseded Paganism, among the Anglo-Saxons; and that kists very like those of Keiss are found containing iron and even Christian relics. But in these cases there is something to mark the influence of Christianity, which is entirely wanting in the older kists. The head is laid towards the west, so as to catch the first glimpse of the Saviour's rising in the east; the arms or legs are frequently crossed, and the cross figured on the grave; and, above all, the contents of the grave, if there are any, show a knowledge of iron and a state of civilization corresponding to the period. None of these circumstances occur in the Keiss kists. The heads lay sometimes north, oftener south, but never west; the arms and legs are never crossed, and not a vestige of any Christian emblem or influence appeared in any of the ten or twelve kists examined.

But it is idle to argue a question which can be decided by an appeal to *facts*. The *fact* is that in the two northern counties, at any rate, of Orkney and Caithness, the graves which may be safely pronounced to be the oldest—from their being on the natural surface of the ground, and covered with simple grass mounds or long barrows; and still more conclusively from their containing only rude stone weapons without sepulchral urns or metals—are in many instances similar to those of Keiss; *i.e.* consisting of an extended kist of flag-stones set on edge. I state this fact on the authority of my friend Mr. George Petrie, of Kirkwall,* who is better acquainted with the antiquities of Orkney than any man living. Nor is other authority wanting to controvert the statement that extended kists belong exclusively to the early Christian period. Dr. Daniel Wilson, in his Pre-historic Scotland, in describing the contracted kists in which the warrior was interred, seated, with his weapons at his side, as those most commonly found underneath ancient cairns and tumuli, expressly adds, "that some few kists of full proportions belong to a period *prior* to this custom;" and "that examples of a full-sized kist with the enclosed skeleton extended at length are met with under circumstances, and attended with relics, which leave no doubt that they belong to both of the primitive periods."

The result of Mr. Bateman's extensive researches in ancient British tumuli, of which an abstract is given by Sir John Lubbock in the Transactions of the Ethnological Society, vol. iii., p. 310, confirms the conclusion that extended sepulture, though more common in the age of Iron, was not confined to one period, several instances being given where it was found in exclusive connection both with bronze and stone. It must be remembered also that such slight sepulchral remains of a barbarous aboriginal race as are indicated by the Caithness kists, would be the first to disappear in settled and cultivated districts; so that the fact of contracted sepulture in megalithic kists being shown as a

* Since writing the above, the Rev. Mr. Joass, who has explored many tumuli in Ross-shire, tells me that the only instance in which he found a rude flint arrow, unaccompanied by any metal or funeral urn, was in an extended kist with an unburnt skeleton.

general rule in the earliest existing remains in southern Britain, does not disprove the possibility of a simpler mode of burial having prevailed during part of the long period which must have elapsed between the earliest cromlech and the first occupation of the British Islands by man in the drift period.

A striking instance of such primæval extended kists is given in the Proceedings of the Society of Scottish Antiquaries (vol. ii., p. 251), where several stone kists are described, which were discovered at Ardyne, near Castle Toward, Argyleshire, and are exact counterparts of my Caithness kists.

ARDYNE KIST.

	Ft.	in.
Length (inside)	5	2
Width	1	3
Height	1	1

This kist contained an extended male skeleton with a rude flint spear-head; and several other similar kists are described bearing every mark of extreme antiquity.

I have dwelt at some length on this point of the extended sepulture, because it has been urged by some eminent antiquaries in a way which seems to me subversive of all rules of evidence. Because extended sepulture in stone kists was practised in early Christian times, is there such an irresistible presumption that this most obvious and simple mode of burial could never have been practised previously, as to compel us to admit the most glaring anomalies, such as the existence of a race of rude limpet-eating savages ignorant of metals in the days of St. Columbus, in districts which had been for centuries previously the seats of a comparatively civilized people, who reared massive tombs and temples, placed the ashes of the dead in sepulchral urns, and manufactured elegant weapons and ornaments of bronze?

In the Life of St. Columbus it is stated that the Saint chancing to meet a Prince of the Orkneys at the palace of King Brude, commended to his care some monks who had lately sailed to the northern seas, and the missionaries afterwards owed their lives to his intercession. The theory that all extended kists necessarily show Christian influence, leads to the absurd supposition that the savage who lay in the extended kist at Keiss, with his rude stone weapons by his side, and a handful of limpets for his food in another world, may have been the identical prince who visited the Court of Scotland, conversed with St. Columbus, and entertained his missionaries.

For my own part, I feel satisfied that under the particular circumstances of this case, the simple mode of sepulture does not militate with the evidence of primitive antiquity from other sources, and specially from the rudeness of the stone and bone implements and absence of metals.

The total want of metals may, I think, be certainly inferred from the entire absence both of metals themselves, and of forms of stone or bone showing the influence of metals in such an extensive series of remains as were discovered in the kists and middens. There are twenty-eight weapons from four several kists, and upwards of a hundred weapons and implements from the middens, and the solitary instances of metal (except two or three nails from the merely superficial sand), are the shears of bronze and iron, and iron pin, which came from the upper midden of the Harbour mound, which was evidently connected with the last stage of occupation at the highest level, by inhabitants civilized enough to have converted the old doorway of the circular fort into a fireplace with a chimney.

Indeed, the evidence goes further, and proves not only the absence of metals but the absence of all stone except that of the district. In the more advanced Stone period instances are frequent in which the presence of finely-wrought weapons of flint, greenstone, porphyry, and other hard stones in districts where Nature provides no such materials, testifies to some degree of intercourse with foreign parts. Nothing of the sort occurs in these Caithness mounds. On the contrary, it is evident that these aborigines were strictly confined to the products of their own beaches for their tools and weapons. They knew the value of flint, as is shown by the numerous flint chips; but having no flints but the small rounded pebbles of some chalk formation which has long since been washed away, and which are not large enough to make serviceable tools or weapons, they were compelled to use the sandstone of the district for the weapons even of their chiefs.

This of itself shows their isolated condition, and that they could not have come in contact with more advanced races. It makes it improbable also that they could have been degenerate descendants of more civilized races, or a band of emigrants or outcasts; as we can hardly imagine a people resting satisfied with such rude knives and arrows of bone and sandstone, whose ancestors had brought with them better forms and materials. The invention of the barb, for instance, to the arrow is one hardly likely to be lost, if once known; and the flints of Caithness, though small, would often have sufficed for the manufacture of barbed arrowheads. The bone arrow-heads also might easily have been barbed, and the stone axes and hammers pierced or grooved for attachment to a handle, had such arts ever been known.

Mr. Christy, whose authority stands so deservedly high with regard to the arts and implements of primitive races, has made a very ingenious supposition, viz., that these relics may belong to a race who.had relapsed into the barbarism of a Stone period from the privation of metals in this remote corner of Britain, as happened to the ancient Danish colonists in Greenland, when severed by the accumulation of ice from all communication with metal-producing countries.

But in the very interesting remains from Greenland which show the gradual retrogression to the use of stone, the improved forms derived from a knowledge of metals are preserved; and it seems to me impossible to account for such excessive rudeness of form as prevails among the weapons of the Caithness kists on any other supposition than that of primæval barbarism.

There is, however, one fact which may argue the knowledge of more advanced arts by these Caithness savages, than would be denoted by their tools and weapons, viz., the occasional presence of the small perforated balls of stone or bone, which are commonly known as "whorls," and supposed to be used with the distaff for spinning. It is true that some authorities doubt their having been used for spinning, and Daniel Wilson in his Pre-historic Scotland contends that they were personal ornaments, relying on their form being often ill-adapted for spinning, and their being found with other rude ornaments interred with male skeletons. Still the resemblance is such to whorls actually used for spinning by savage races, as to afford a strong inference that this was their destination; if so, the presence of a "whorl" implies a knowledge of the art of spinning.

The evidence, however, is very doubtful. If the "whorls" often resemble those actually used in spinning, they equally resemble those certainly used for ornament. There are numerous necklaces and collars in the British Museum, the Copenhagen Museum, and other antiquarian collections, composed of perforated stones, pieces of clay and bone, in no respect distinguishable from common whorls. Glass beads of precisely the same size and pattern were made at a later period, which were undoubtedly intended for ornament and not for spinning.

If to this we add that whorls have often been found with male skeletons, and that the form and want of density of those made of porous bone often rendered them very unsuitable for spinning, the balance of argument seems to incline in favour of Dr. Wilson's view. There is, moreover, one other argument which to my mind carries considerable force, viz., that in secluded districts where the use of the distaff has been continued almost down to the present day, no idea seems to be entertained that the whorls, which are occasionally picked up, are in any way connected with spinning.

In Cornwall they are known as "Pixies grindstones," and in Lewis a curious account is given by Captain Thomas in the Proceedings of the Society of Scottish Antiquaries, vol. iv., p. 119, of the popular belief that they are what are called "snake-stones," or formed by a succession of snakes creeping through the same hole, and hardening the dust into stone by the slime exuding from their bodies. It is evident therefore, that the whorls stand in the same category as the flint arrow-heads or elf-bolts, as objects the use of which has been long since forgotten, and which have passed into the domain of myth; a conclusion which is hardly reconcileable with the supposition that they have always accompanied the distaff.

I may add that no whorls were found in any of the kists, and most of them came from the upper strata of the middens; but some came from the middle or secondary middens; and I cannot say positively that one or two may not have come from the lower middens, as unfortunately my attention had not been sufficiently called to the point to enable me to identify the exact position in which every whorl was found.

There remains, therefore, at the utmost some slight presumption that the primæval savages of the kists may have known the art of spinning, though further research will be required to determine this point conclusively.

FAUNA.—By the kind aid of Mr. Roberts and Mr. Carter Blake, who have been assisted in their identifications by Mr. Davies, of the British Museum, I am enabled to give the following complete list of the animal remains of the Keiss middens. We are indebted to Professor Owen for the important identification of the *Alca impennis* or Great Auk.

Mollusca:—Limpet (*Patella vulgaris*); periwinkle (*Littorina litorea*); lesser periwinkle (*Littorina nontridia*); whelk (*Buccinum undatum*); cockle (*Cardium*); scallop (*Pecten majus*); lesser scallop (*Pecten Argus*).

Annulosa:—Lobster (*Serpula*).

Fish:—Cod (*Morrhua vulgata*).

Mammalia:—Ox (*Bos longifrons*): horse (*Equus caballus* (?) *fossilis*); red deer (*Cervus elephas*); goat (*Capra hircus*); hog (*Sus serofa*); dog (*Canis familiaris* or *familiaris fossilis*); fox (*Canis vulpes*); rabbit (*Lupus cuniculus*), perhaps recent.

Cetacea:—Grampus (*Delphinus orca*), or small whale; dolphin (*Delphinus dolphis*), or some other small cetacean.

Birds:—Great auk (*Alca impennis*): lesser auk (*Alca tarda*); cormorant (*Philacrocorax carbo*); shag (*Philacrocorax graculus*); solon goose (*Sula bassana*).

The most interesting fact is the discovery of the "Alca impennis," which is now extinct in Europe, having but lately died out in Iceland, but said to survive in Greenland. Its bones are frequent in the Danish Kjökkenmöddings, where they have been thought to imply great antiquity and a more glacial climate, but it is believed that they have never been found in any tumuli or deposits of a later date than these primæval middens. Hence their discovery in the Caithness middens affords an important link of connection with those of Denmark, and strengthens the evidence of high antiquity drawn from the rudeness of the implements.

The fauna also corresponds with that of the Danish middens in its general characters, and contains just such an assemblage of animals as are commonly found in quaternary

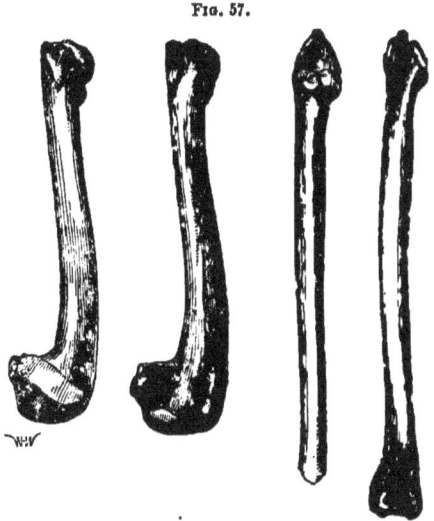

FIG. 57.

Bones of Alca impennis. ½ nat. size.

deposits. The dog is the only one of which we may assume with some certainty that it was in the domestic state. I found this conjecture mainly on the jaw found in one of the kists, apparently of the hunter's faithful dog to bear him company; but the size corresponds either to that of a large shepherd's dog, or of the fossil dog of the quaternary period; and if dogs were domesticated, it is singular that so few remains should be found, and no trace of the gnawing of other bones, which is so common in the Danish middens. The ox was the *bos longifrons*; the hog probably wild, from the size of the tusks; the horse, a large-headed animal of small size, but considerably larger than the Shetland pony, corresponding perfectly with the *Equus fossilis*, and probably wild, as it had been commonly used for food; the goat precisely similar to the fossil goat from the newer pliocene figured by Owen in his "British Fossil Mammals."

The absence of the sheep strengthens the inference against domesticated animals; and the horns of the red deer confirm the supposition of considerable antiquity, some of them being of unusually large size and very abnormal (fig. 58). It will be

FIG. 58.

Red Deer's Horn. ⅓ nat. size.

recollected that in the earliest lake-dwellings of the age of stone in Switzerland the goats outnumbered the sheep, but towards the close of the same period the sheep were more abundant than the goats. The presence of goats without sheep, therefore, in the Caithness middens, points to a connection rather with the antecedent Danish middens than with the earliest relics of the Stone period in Switzerland, agreeing completely with the similar evidence derived from the presence of the *Alca impennis* and the excessive rudeness of the stone and bone implements.

I have since heard of the bone of a sheep having been found in one of these mounds; but as it came from the surface it can hardly be relied on to disprove the inference from the numerous jaws and other remains of goats which come from the body of the several middens, though I should fully expect that sheep's bones would be often found in such situations, as they must frequently have been occupied down to a date when the sheep was common in the North of Scotland, even if it be true that the goat only was known in the earliest period.

More extensive researches, however, are requisite to establish trustworthy conclusions as to the nature of the fauna of the Scottish middens, and its relations to those of the Danish Kjökkenmöddings and Swiss Lacustrine dwellings. For the present all we can say is, that as far as the evidence now goes the presumption is against a knowledge of the domesticated animals, except the dog; and that there is a considerable general resemblance to the fauna of the Danish Kjökkenmöddings. If the identification of the Caithness remains with those of the wild and not the domestic varieties should be confirmed, they would be identical with those of the Kjökkenmöddings, with the following not very material exceptions. The *bos urus* of Denmark is replaced by the *bos longifrons*; the horse and goat are present; and the bear, lynx, beaver, and marten are wanting. But as both horse and goat existed in a wild state in Britain before and after the glacial period, their presence in such a collection does not invalidate its general character, unless it can be shown that the remains are of the domestic species.

On the other hand, some of the points of resemblance between the fauna of the Danish and North British Kjökkenmöddings are very remarkable. I have referred to the presence of the "Alca impennis" in each. In each the stag genus is represented by the red deer, often of larger size than any now existing, to the exclusion of the reindeer, which figures so prominently in the cave period in latitudes much further south.

FOOD.—This was evidently composed principally of shell-fish from the adjoining shore, consisting in nine cases out of ten of periwinkles and limpets. Fish and whales were also eaten, but the latter were probably stranded. Even as regards fish, the total absence of anything like fish-hooks or tackle, and the very small proportion of fish bones on a coast abounding with fish, suggests a doubt whether they did more than pick up dead fish which are very frequently cast up on this shore.

I never heard of canoes, which are so common further south, being found in any of the peat mosses or lake marls of Caithness or Orkney, and although the country was doubtless once covered with a scrubby underwood, I question if trees of sufficient magnitude to form canoes ever existed in sufficient number near the sea-shore or navigable rivers to teach the savages the art of boat-building. Be this as it may, the fact is worth noticing that in these refuse heaps on the shore of a sea abounding in fish, there are fewer bones of fish than of *Bos longifrons*, and no traces of any fishing or boating tackle. In this respect the contrast is remarkable with the Danish Kjökkenmöddings, in which, as stated by Sir John Lubbock, the fish bones are "almost innumerable."

The fauna enumerated all afforded food, the whole of the remains having been found in the middens, and in many cases showing the action of fire. The two instances of human jaws found in the middens afford a strong presumption that cannibalism was occasionally resorted to. Shellfish only being placed in the kists as food for the dead, strengthens the presumption that they were the staple and ordinary article of food. Of the mammalian remains those of goat and ox were most numerous; then pig, horse, and stag; and of dog and fox a single specimen only of each was found.

Did grain form any part of their food? Upon this point there is no sufficient evidence. In two cases large stones* were found, nearly circular, in which holes had been bored on opposite sides to a certain depth, as if an attempt had

* See Plate vii., fig. 9.

been made to bore a central hole which had been abandoned. These may have been intended for quern stones, and if so, grain was probably used. But there is no proof that these were quern stones; on the contrary, they seem unsuited for such a purpose, from their imperfect circular form and want of density and hardness, and one at least of these stones showed traces of the action of fire, and was covered with greasy black ashes and decomposed animal matter.

A large stone block was found with a space excavated in it, which, if circular, might have been the lower stone of a small quern, but it was oblong and apparently intended as a mortar in which to pound with the oval sandstone beach stones used as hammers.

Grain may have been so pounded, but it is equally possible that bones may have been thus reduced to the small splinters in which they are generally found, for the sake of extracting the marrow. I looked carefully among the ashes and débris for any trace of grain or vegetable substance, but could never find anything but small pieces of wood charcoal; and for the present all that can be said is that there is no proof of the use of grain, and some assumption against it from the absence of unmistakeable querns which are so common in connection with later buildings.

The attrition of the teeth may possibly afford an argument; but I apprehend that this might equally result from gnawing bones and eating large quantities of shell-fish mixed with sand.

The absence of animal bones in any of the kists would seem to imply that the capture of a wild ox or stag was a rare event, and to strengthen the inference against a knowledge of domestic animals, as otherwise we might have expected to find something better than limpets and periwinkles in the tomb of a chief.

I think an increase in the number of animal remains was

discernible in the upper middens, as if the power of capturing wild animals had increased with an improvement in the weapons of chase. Stags' horns especially were certainly more numerous in the upper portions of the mounds. A large proportion of the larger animals had been young, as shown by the presence of the milk teeth, which may lead to the inference that with such very imperfect weapons the savages could seldom succeed in killing an adult. This further strengthens the presumption that the remains are of wild animals, as the domestic horse, for instance, would have been too valuable to kill for food while young.

On the whole the diet of this people seems to have been very like that of the savages of Tierra del Fuego, so admirably described by Darwin in his "Voyage of a Naturalist," as consisting mainly of shell-fish with an occasional feast on a stranded whale or captured guanaco.

The apparent connection between the ancient shell-middens and the burgs or circular towers, shown by the Harbour Mound, is one of the most interesting features of the present discoveries. These burgs, whose remains are so common in the North of Scotland, have usually been assigned to a very recent period. Although built of unhewn stones the masonry is so massive and regular that they have the appearance of being the fortresses of a comparatively civilized and warlike people, and in fact we know that they were used as such by the Scandinavians as late as the ninth century. Torfæus relates that Erlend carried off the mother of Harold, Earl of Orkney, who was famed for her beauty, to the Burg of Mousa in Shetland, where he was unsuccessfully besieged by the Earl, who after a time came to terms with Erlend, finding the fort impregnable. It seems difficult to believe that such forts could have been built by the limpet-eating savages, whose tools and weapons were ruder than those of the caverns of Les Eyzies or the drifts of Abbeville.

And yet such seems to be the evidence of the section of the Harbour Mound. It is of course possible that the building may be posterior to the lower and more ancient midden, and that the wall may have been sunk through it to the natural rock to obtain a more secure foundation. But the appearances hardly favoured such a supposition, especially as the two other concentric walls, which were unquestionably later additions, were not carried down to a lower level than that of their respective floors, and had evidently been built on the accumulated midden and rubbish of the original structure. Further investigation is necessary to clear up the point; but in the meantime there is a good deal of evidence to show that the burgs really date back to a very remote period.

The hypothesis of a Scandinavian origin is conclusively refuted by the fact, vouched for by the high authority of Worsaae and Munch, that nothing at all resembling them is to be found in any Scandinavian country. The local names, also so common in Orkney and Shetland, in which "burg" enters, show clearly that these burgs existed when the names were given by the Scandinavian invaders.

Wilson, in his "Pre-historic Scotland," after reviewing the evidence respecting the burgs, states his opinion that they are the work of a people "whose arts were extremely rude," and he attributes their erection to a period "long prior to the earliest recorded traces of Scandinavian invasion."

I am enabled to state some still more conclusive evidence of the high antiquity of the burgs on the authority of Mr. George Petrie, of Kirkwall.

At the Burg of Okstro, in the parish of Birsa, Orkney, graves of the Bronze period were discovered in the superficial soil of a green mound, which was itself the remains of a ruined burg. There could be no mistake here as to the facts or the order of succession. Bronze rings and other ornaments were found with urns containing burnt human bones of the usual type of the Bronze period, in stone kists scattered over the surface of a green hillock at a depth of two or three feet from the surface. On digging deeper into the mound the foundations of a massive circular burg were disclosed, with a wall twelve feet thick, inclosing an area of forty-five feet in diameter, with other concentric walls and a subterranean well or chamber, in connection with which were found several very rude implements of stone and bone, some deer's horns with marks of cutting on them, and extremely coarse pottery. In other words, an assemblage of objects closely corresponding with those of the Keiss Harbour Burg.

The Burgs of Burray, Hoxay, Burghar, and various other Orkney Burgs, have furnished a similar collection of objects; for instance, that of Burray contained several rude stone vessels resembling lamps or mortars; circular perforated stones and pieces of bone (whorls); bone cup made of a whale's vertebra; five bone combs; two bone pins; several pointed bones with and without heads; bone arrow-heads; and worked deer's horn.

Although I have had no opportunity myself of exploring with sufficient care any of the numerous shell-mounds and middens in Orkney; yet a cursory examination of several of them enables me to say that they correspond entirely in character with those I have described in Caithness. In each case periwinkles and limpets form the staple of the midden, with the addition of cockles and oysters in some of the sheltered bays where these molluscs are now found; remains are common of either sheep or goat, ox (*bos longifrons*), red deer, and pig, with occasional horse, dog, and fox; rude oval beach stones used as hammers, and circular slingstones, are the commonest form of stone implement; rude pins or skewers of bone are frequent; and the fragments of pottery are of the same coarse hand-made description. The only difference I have observed is that fish bones are certainly more abundant in some of the Orkney middens which stand on the shores of sheltered bays. These middens are in some cases associated with burgs, in others with Picts' houses or subterranean chambers, and in others stand alone without any remaining trace of building.

The only reason why the evidence that such burgs as the above belong to the Stone period has not been accepted as conclusive is, that objects of a later date as bronze, gold, and even iron, have been occasionally found with those of an earlier type. But, as I have had so often occasion to urge, the mere fact of the occasional presence of a modern object in a site which has beyond all doubt been successively occupied down to a recent period, proves little or nothing. A solitary bronze ornament was found in the débris of the Burg of Okstro. Mr. Petrie believes this fell from the kists above. This supposition, in itself highly probable, reconciles all the facts; while how can we account otherwise for the kists of the Bronze period being on the surface of the mound, and for the anomaly of a people acquainted with bronze having such extremely rude implements of stone, bone, and pottery.

We know that the Scandinavians sometimes occupied these burgs for purposes of dwelling and defence, as in the case of Mousa, and if so, how could we do otherwise than discover occasional weapons and implements of iron, mixed up with the relics of the primitive inhabitants. It is well ascertained, moreover, that the Scandinavians often selected old ruined burgs as burying-places, and buried with the dead as charms relics which they had found of older periods, such as the so-called Elfin arrows, and Thor's hammers or celts, thus adding to the apparent confusion of the Stone, Bronze, and Iron periods. Further evidence of the great antiquity of many of the Orcadian Burgs is afforded by the fact that in several cases a great part of the original circle has disappeared by the retreat of the coast line in situations so sheltered that the present low cliff or terrace is rarely touched even by the most violent gales.

On the whole, therefore, I see no difficulty in assigning a high antiquity to many of these burgs, and considering these primitive structures to have been the work of the people, whoever they were, who reared the Stones of Stenness, constructed the Picts' Houses, and covered the northern counties and islands of Scotland with their graves, long prior to the general introduction of metals or the advent of any historical race. But the difficulty remains how a people so savage as is shown by their food and implements, could have raised structures so massive and enduring. To this I can only observe that the civilization of a primitive people seems to depend very much on the materials with which Nature has supplied them. Where Nature gave plenty of sharp flints, but no sea beach with stones suitable for buildings, as in the Valleys of the South of France, where man lived contemporary with the reindeer, he dwelt in caverns but attained to considerable skill and even taste in the art of decorative carving. In Caithness and Orkney, again, these conditions were exactly reversed. The sandstone of the district gave a material so bad for cutting purposes that the weapons and tools of the primitive savages, and all arts and ornaments depending on cutting tools, remained at the lowest ebb; while on the other hand Nature provided a boundless profusion of flags and blocks regularly squared for building, and supplied the means, while by the inclemency of the climate and absence of shelter in woods or caves she afforded the inducement, to develope the innate constructive faculty in the direction of architecture.

I have often thought that the instinct of children affords

some clue to that of savages; and on these sea shores I have
seen children, tempted by the facility of selecting stones of
regular form, build in sport very substantial miniature round
towers, of a form not unlike that of the ancient burg. In
fact, the solid circular tower is a simple idea which could
hardly fail to occur to a people, however savage, who felt the
want of shelter and defence, and had plenty of squared
blocks and flags ready to their hand; and the modifications
of a second concentric wall and converging roofs are natural
developments of the original idea to provide shelter where
large timber was probably wanting. To realize the position
of primæval man in Caithness we must recollect that he had
abundance of stone but little wood; and that his cutting
tools and weapons were as inferior to those of the flint-using
Esquimaux as these, again, are to the iron implements of the
modern European. Such a people might build solid towers
while they remained ignorant of fish-hooks and barbed arrow-
heads, and never attempted to carve ornaments on the handles of their knives or lances.

Another consideration with reference to the burgs is that
in assigning them to the Stone period an immense duration,
comprising many changes, must be assigned to the Stone
period itself. It probably extended in Britain from the
commencement of the Quaternary period, while these islands
were still united to the continent, to within ten or twenty
centuries of the Christian era. During this vast period, in
comparison with which the historical and semi-historical
ages of Iron and Bronze dwindle to a point, how many must
have been the vicissitudes. The single fact of the existence of
such a structure as the Stones of Stenness with their accompanying monuments, tells us of a population sufficiently
dense and civilized to be swayed by priests, and led by
religious ideas to attempt vast undertakings. What the
Pyramids were to Egypt, the Stones of Stenness must have

been to a once numerous people, the ruins of whose graves and dwellings meet the ploughshare in almost every field in the remote Orkneys, but of whom all historical traces and even traditions have disappeared as completely as of the mound-builders of the Mississippi.

Unknown ages may have elapsed in a state of savagery too dense and animal-like to leave records; until some fortunate impulse from without, or improvement from within, raised the race to the level where they buried their dead in kists and raised tumuli and dwellings, at first simple and humble, but by degrees more massive and complicated, until at length the Stone civilization culminated in such national monuments and temples as the circles of Stonehenge and Stenness.

TYPE OF RACE.—The valuable memoir which Professor Huxley has been kind enough to subjoin, places the anatomical facts fully before the scientific world, and it only remains for me to add a few general remarks.

It is a most important and interesting fact that in association with these very rude and primitive remains a type of human race should have been discovered so savage and degraded, as to present more resemblance to the lowest Australian than to any historical European race. Authorities may differ as to the precise degree of the analogies which Prof. Huxley points out between these Caithness crania and those of the ancient river-beds and recent Australians, but there can be no second opinion as to the general facts. The difference of cranial type between a savage and a civilized race consists broadly in the approximation of the former to the animal type. There is generally less volume of brain, always a much less proportion of it in front. The bony framework of the skull preponderates more over the inclosed brain. The jaws project more, the ridges and processes for muscular attachment are more strongly marked. Now in all these particulars the type, of which the Caithness skull No. 1 is the extreme example, is far more animal-like than that of any European race either known in history or hitherto discovered in pre-historic tombs of the Iron, Bronze, or later Stone periods. If a line be drawn vertically over the skull from ear to ear, half the brain lies in front of such a line in any average well-formed European head; while the proportion is not one-fourth in the Keiss skulls. The degree of prognathism, as shown by the projection of the upper jaw and teeth, and the narrowness of the ape-like palate, is equal to that of the lowest specimens of the Negro and Australian races.

In other anatomical peculiarities, so ably pointed out by Prof. Huxley, and more especially in the anomalous formation of the pelvis, the difference from any known European type and resemblance to, or rather exaggeration of, the rudest Australian type, is equally remarkable.

No one can doubt that we have here an extremely savage type. No one can doubt that among the family of savage types the analogies are altogether with the Negro as opposed to the Mongol; and that this tribe of aboriginal Britons must have much more closely resembled the Australian or Tasmanian than the Laplander or Esquimaux.

Thus far the evidence favours the views of the advocates of progressive development. The theory which might appear best suited to the facts would be that the human type is that of the first men who, while Britain was yet united with a southern continent, migrated northwards as the rigour of the glacial period subsided, with the other fauna of the quaternary period: that this race, whose skulls are occasionally found in caves and river-beds, lived on for an indefinite period little changed, until they were exterminated, or enslaved and assimilated, by superior races in times approaching to the historical era, leaving, however, small fragments in remote and secluded situations who preserved the primitive type and savage rudeness down to a period sufficiently modern to allow of their relics being occasionally discovered. The whole story would then be consistent—strangeness and extreme rudeness of weapons and implements would correspond with strangeness and extreme rudeness of human type.

A fauna, corresponding generally with that of the Danish Kjökkenmöddings would point to an antiquity sufficient to give ample time for all requisite successions or modifications of race. We could picture to ourselves some still ruder cranial form of the early drift period gradually developing itself into the river-bed type and thence into the Kumbo-Kephalic, which so many of the best authorities believe to be the primitive British type. The invasion of a Brachycephalic race, more advanced in the arts though still within the Stone period, might be supposed to form a mixed people, who either attained to the civilization of the first historical Britons, by their own development, aided by intercourse with the Phœnician and other foreign traders; or who were themselves again subjugated by fresh races of invaders acquainted with the metals.

It is evident, however, that the time has not yet come when we can safely venture on such complete and symmetrical theories. The Neanderthal skull had scarcely begun to popularize the theory of progressive human development, before the accurate measurements of that of Engis proved that men nowise differing from modern Europeans were contemporaries of the cave-bear and tiger.

In like manner the evidence of the Keiss skeletons is greatly neutralized by the very remarkable fact that while the majority approximate to the Australian savage, one at least is a fair specimen of an ancient Briton differing in no essential respect from a modern European.

It is extremely difficult to account for a fact which antecedently would have appeared so improbable. Even if we were to ignore the evidence derived from the low type of most of the skulls, and consider these as accidental varieties, the still more conclusive proofs remain from the rudeness of the implements and nature of the fauna. These denote an era, if not of absolute time at any rate of relative progress and civilization, below that of the ordinary British barrows and cromlechs, below even the oldest lake-dwellings of Switzerland, and similar in many respects to that of the Danish Kjökkenmöddings. Our knowledge of the distribution of cranial types both in space and time is far too imperfect to enable us to place any conjectural evidence derived from them in opposition to the positive evidence of contemporaneous relics. The Engis skull might have been taken for that of a modern Belgian, and those of the Stone period in Switzerland for modern Helvetians, if they had not been associated with remains which proved their antiquity.

We must take the age, therefore, of the Keiss graves from their rude stone and bone implements and primitive fauna, and accommodate as we best can the fact that the human remains show types so widely different. One solution would be to suppose, that there really had been an intermixture of two entirely distinct races. But it seems difficult to believe that such an intermixture could have taken place without some advance in the arts and weapons, and some relative superiority of the European over the Australoid type. But in this case, the man with the British type of skull was neither chief nor slave, but lay in an ordinary kist with a rude stone hammer and handful of limpets by his side, just like one of the other savages. He may have been a refugee or captive, or the descendant of such, but even in this case it is difficult to account for the excessive rudeness of the weapons. Intercourse with any foreign tribes or countries, however slight, must, one would have imagined, have led to some knowledge of a better material than the native sandstone, and some improvement in the form of the lances and arrow-heads on which they depended for their daily subsistence. Instances, however, are not wanting in Australia where such occasional intercourse has taken place without altering the habits of the savages, although its effects may be traced in the cranial forms of some of their descendants.

In the very interesting account of the Australian aborigines by Mr. A. Oldfield in the Transactions of the Ethnological Society, New Series, vol. iii., p. 218, the following passage occurs, which may possibly throw some light on the question. "At Champion Bay, in Western Australia, I was much surprised to find in some of the *old* natives features approaching the European type, although these parts had been settled but a very few years. I mentioned this fact to a medical gentleman, who informed me that he had made the same observation, and could account for it in no other way than by supposing that a ship which had sailed from Calcutta to Swan River in the early days of the colony, and had never since been heard of, was lost in these parts, and that some of her people who had escaped had mingled with this tribe, a surmise strengthened by the traditions of the natives, who to this day call Perth (the capital of Western Australia) Ca-cat-ta, having probably mistaken the place of departure for that of the destination of the rescued people; added to this they often asserted that in the event of the departure of the whites from among them, there were many of their females whom their laws would permit them to eat, they having white blood in their veins. This approach to the European type of features I have also observed among the natives about Geographe Bay, where the unfortunate Dr. Vasse was so cruelly deserted by his inhuman superior. According to the account of these natives, this unhappy naturalist lived many years among them, conforming to all their habits, and at length dying a natural death."

Some such accident may possibly have thrown on the coasts of Caithness a few isolated individuals of superior race, from the southern parts of the island, before any wave of conquest extended their dominion to the extreme north and introduced, with superior arts, those relations of slavery of the inferior race of which we find traces in some of the Orkney tumuli. I know of two instances in which kists were found there containing two skeletons, one of which had been apparently laid first in the grave and disposed with care, while the other had been huddled in at the feet of the former. In each case the skull of the first skeleton was of the superior or ancient British type, while that of the other or presumed slave, was very similar to the degraded Keiss type.

The only other supposition is that the two types may have developed themselves spontaneously in the same race. In favour of this it may be said that the river-bed type, which is probably the original one, is in some respects intermediate between the extreme forms. Lengthen it out and narrow it, and it approximates to the Australoid No. 1; improve its frontal development and diminish its prognathism, and it approximates to the ancient British No. 7. But it would be difficult without more evidence than we at present possess of intermediate forms shading off the various gradations between No. 1 and No. 7, to admit that what Professor Huxley calls "the most remarkably degraded European skull which has hitherto been discovered" is of the same family as one which "differs in no important respect from a well-formed Englishman of the present day;" especially when we find the difference of cranial characters confirmed by the still more remarkable differences of pelvic conformation, and that not in one instance only but in several.

The result of recent researches is certainly rather to establish the existence of two distinct primitive types in Europe at the earliest known period. The comprehensive review of the mass of facts accumulated by recent explorations of tumuli and sepulchral caves in Britain and France, by Dr. Thurnam in his Memoir "On the Two principal Forms of Ancient British and Gaulish Skulls," published in the Anthropological Society's Memoirs, vol. i., appears to establish certain conclusions which have an important bearing on the questions raised by the Keiss crania.

In England the distinction is well marked between the skulls of a tall race of brachycephalic type, which are found in round barrows of the Later Stone or Bronze age, and those of an earlier and less robust dolichocephalic race, which are found in the primary interments of chambered tumuli and long barrows, associated with nothing but rude implements of stone and bone. So marked and uniform is the distinction that Dr. Thurnam lays down the axiom—*Long barrows, long skulls; round barrows, round or short skulls.*

The Keiss crania confirm this axiom, as they are all more or less long skulls, and come from a long barrow; which, from the associated remains, belongs to a very rude and primitive Stone period. They differ, however, from the primitive English dolichocephali described by Dr. Thurnam, firstly, by showing in some specimens a much more savage and degraded type, characterised by extreme prognathism; secondly, by furnishing other specimens of a very superior type.

But in this respect they find plenty of parallels on the Continent, and thus add another link to those discoveries which tend gradually to unite the scattered facts relating to the early history of man into one harmonious whole. In France, the evidence from numerous tumuli of the Stone period establishes the simultaneous existence of two races.

Dr. Thurnam thus sums up the evidence derived from accurate measurements of the crania of a large number of tumuli:—"So far as our knowledge of the skull-forms of the people of ancient Gaul extends, the table before us shows a mixture, in the same tomb, of the long and short types, such as certainly does not occur in the ancient British barrows of England. Conclusive proof of priority of a dolichocephalous race, in the order of succession, has not yet been obtained for Gaul. On the contrary, two races—one dolichocephalous, the other brachycephalous—appear to have come into contact in that country at a very early epoch; and apparently, during the later Stone period, were more or less mixed or blended. Which of the two first occupied the soil of Gaul, further researches must determine, though the presumption is in favour of its having been the dolichocephalous, as was clearly the case in Britain."

Vogt even goes so far as to say that in France "the further we go back the greater is the contrast between individual types;" and the description of several of the crania given by Thurnam goes far to bear out this assertion. The contrast between the Keiss skulls, No. 1 and No. 7, is scarcely greater than that between the skull No. 209 *bis* of the Paris Museum from Bougon (Deux Sevres), distinguished "by great depression of the very retrocedent frontal, and extreme negro-like prognathism; the intermaxillaries projecting almost as in the gorilla," and the Lombrive skull of the Reindeer period, which Vogt truly calls "on the whole a noble one:" or between the extremely dolichocephalous and extremely brachycephalous skulls found in the same sepulchres at Nogent and at Orrony.

The same contrast seems to exist, in a greater or less degree, between the skulls of the Early Stone period throughout the Continent of Europe. Those of Scandinavia are decidedly brachycephalic; but even in the tombs of Borreby and Moen, nearly one-fourth of the whole number deviate from that type, and a few are dolichocephalic.

The Neanderthal and Engis skulls are dolichocephalic, which seems to be the general type of the early cave skulls of Belgium and Germany, though there are some instances of the opposite type; while in Switzerland the oldest type seems to be, like that of the modern Swiss, square-headed; with some instances of very long and narrow skulls, known as "Apostle skulls," and thought to be of a later period.

On the whole, the tendency of opinion seems to be towards the conclusion that as the Quaternary geological period in Europe shows traces of two distinct influences in its fauna— one African, as shown by the remains of the hippopotamus, elephant, and large carnivora; the other Arctic, as shown by those of the Siberian mammoth and musk ox, and most conclusively by the presence of the reindeer in the South of France—so does it disclose in the earliest traces of man yet discovered two distinct types, one presumably of Southern, the other of Northern origin.

The great Iberian family, of which an isolated branch still survives among the Basques, seems to have been of the same race as the Berbers of Northern Africa, and both may be modified descendants of a primitive dolichocephalic population which extended itself northwards, while Western Europe formed one continent with Africa. The discovery by Broca that the Basque type is really dolichocephalic, and not, as formerly supposed, akin to the short-headed Turanian, adds considerable weight to this supposition. The primitive Brachycephali, on the other hand, present a type resembling that of the Turanian races of the North and East, and it can hardly be accidental that skulls resembling those of Fins and Lapps should be found associated with the reindeer and other Arctic animals, wherever their range has extended.

These two primitive barbarous races meeting probably at the same low ebb of civilization, and equally unprovided with efficient weapons, may have occasionally intermingled during the long period of the Stone age, and given rise to intermediate types; while at a later period superior races of Indo-European origin may have partly extirpated and partly assimilated, or been assimilated by, the old races, on whom they imposed their own language.

This, I believe, comes nearest to a theory which would account for the great mass of interesting and often apparently conflicting facts which have been accumulated during the last few years by the labours of so many distinguished men in the various sciences of geology, anthropology, antiquities, and language. On this supposition the Caithness relics described in these pages would be those of a secluded tribe of that branch of the primitive race, whose ancestors were the dolichocephali, or long-headed men of the riverbeds and long barrows or earliest British tombs, with whom a few of the subsequent and superior races had occasionally mingled, but not in sufficient numbers to alter their arts and habits of life.

I have hazarded the above observations because I believe that some degree of theory is necessary to explain facts, and useful in inciting that discussion which leads to their verification. But I am fully sensible that researches into the Scottish Kjökkenmöddings, as extensive and as carefully conducted as into those of Denmark and Switzerland, are required before we can pronounce with confidence on any one of the important points which has been raised in the preceding pages. All I pretend to say is this, that the result of the first considerable exploration of the Kjökkenmöddings of the North of Scotland, which has yet been made with sufficient accuracy, establishes a *primâ facie* case in support of the following propositions—

The succession of a Stone, Bronze, and Iron period, which has been established in Scandinavia and Switzerland, has existed also in Scotland.

The Stone period comprises an early and later period, the former showing a condition of extreme rudeness which connects it in all probability with the earliest race of human inhabitants in Britain.

The character of these remains and of the associated fauna show much analogy with those of the Kjökkenmöddings of Denmark.

The general type of the race, however, appears to have been very different, and to confirm the theory of Wilson and other writers, that the earliest inhabitants of North Britain were Kumbo-cephalic, approximating to a Negroid or Australoid rather than to a Mongolian or Arctic type.

Along with this type, however, appears one of very superior character, similar to that of ordinary ancient Britons, showing that some mixture of races had taken place, while remote tribes still lingered on in the rude conditions of the early Stone period.

No conclusive inference can be drawn from the mode of sepulture, it being proved in several instances that the simple mode of extended interment in a stone kist, covered by a slight mound, which prevailed in early Christian times, was practised also in ages long antecedent by a people ruder and more primitive in their tools, weapons, and food than those who interred their dead in a contracted posture, in massive kists or cromlechs, under more ambitious tumuli.

It only remains in conclusion to add a few remarks in explanation of the subjoined Plates. It seemed to me that the best mode of presenting a summary of the facts relating to these North British Kjökkenmöddings in the way most likely to lead to useful comparison and further discovery, would be to give, in addition to the figures in the text, a series of figures of the most characteristic weapons and implements, classified according to their objects, and showing as far as possible the different types, and the progression from the rudest to the most perfect forms of the same type that were found.

PLATE I.

BATTLE AXE AND SPEAR-HEADS.

FIG. 1. Battle Axe from Chief's Kist.
¼ actual size.

This is a block of hard sandstone of the rudest possible form, showing no traces of chipping or grinding. It is in fact a gigantic flake, apparently struck off at a blow, though it would be a most effective weapon in cleaving the skull of an enemy or wild animal, if used as a chopper in the hand of a brawny savage. It shows so little trace of design that had it not been found in a kist with a number of other weapons, it would certainly have been thrown aside as showing no sufficient proof of having been used or manufactured by man. It is interesting from its dissimilarity to any of the rude forms of axes or celts of the Early Stone period, which have been found elsewhere.

FIG. 2. Spear-head from Chief's Kist.
½ actual size.
FIG. 3. Spear-head from Birkle Hill Kist.
½ actual size.
FIG. 4. Spear-head from Kist No. 9.
½ actual size.
FIG. 5. Spear-head from Kist No. 9.
½ actual size.
FIG. 6. Spear-head from Chief's Kist.
½ actual size.

Of these spear-heads fig. 2 is excessively rude, being chipped roughly on one face only; the others presenting the natural surface of the stone. Fig. 3 is also very slightly chipped into shape. Fig. 4 shows more chipping; and fig. 5 is still more carefully chipped and scraped into shape, and is made to taper at the lower end for insertion into a socket. One of the same pattern as fig. 5, but rather larger, was found in the Harbour Midden. Fig. 6 is of a different type, and has been broken at the point, the dotted lines showing the conjectural restoration.

PLATE II.

Arrow-heads.

Fig. 1. Arrow-head from Chief's Kist.
½ actual size.
Figs. 2, 3. Arrow-head from Kist No. 9.
actual size.
Figs. 4, 5. Arrow-heads or small spear-heads, from Kist No. 9.
actual size.
Figs. 6-8. Arrow-heads of bone from Churchyard and Harbour Middens.
½ actual size.

Figs. 1, 2, and 3 are very rude; fig. 4 is more carefully chipped; and fig. 5 is of improved construction, having been scraped or roughly ground into regular shape, though not polished.

The bone arrow-heads are extremely rude, and must have been very inefficient as weapons.

All these arrow-heads present more or less of the same type as the spear-heads (figs. 2-5, pl. 1), which is more simple and rude than that of any of the five varieties of flint arrow-heads mentioned by Sir W. R. Wilde in his Catalogue of the Museum of Irish Antiquities, having neither barbs, nor any notch, groove, or projection to facilitate attachment to a shaft (except in the case of the bone arrowhead, fig. 8).

The contrast of these to the beautifully finished stone arrows of a later period which are often found in the same district, is most striking.

PLATE III.

KNIVES, SCRAPERS, OR CHISELS.

FIGS. 1–4. Sandstone knives from Chief's Kist.
½ actual size.
FIG. 5. Knife from Harbour Midden.
½ actual size.
FIGS. 6, 7. Knives or scrapers from Chief's Kist.
½ actual size.
FIG. 8. Quartz scraper from Birkle Hill Kist.
½ actual size.
FIG. 9. Knife or scraper of bone from Harbour Midden.
½ actual size.
FIG. 10. Chisel or scraper of bone from Harbour Midden.
½ actual size.

Figs. 1 and 2 are specimens of sandstone knives so very rude and destitute of cutting edge that it is difficult to imagine their use. Had they not been found in kists with other weapons, they could not have been accepted as showing traces of human construction.

Figs. 3–5 are sandstone flakes with a tolerably sharp edge, and figs. 6 and 7, though showing little construction, have a very keen edge, considering the nature of the material, and might have been well used in cutting flesh or hides, or even in cutting fresh bone. I have a fac-simile of fig. 7 from a Kjökkenmödding, near Stronness, Orkney, which tends to show that this form was characteristic of the period. It is, in effect, nothing but a thin flake struck off the flatly circular end of a block of hard sandstone. Fig. 8 was found in a kist with weapons, and being of hard quartz is conjectured to have been used as a scraper to grind the sandstoné spears and knives into shape, and give them a sharp point or edge. A similar one was found in another kist with a small deer's horn handle adjoining, which is figured plate v., fig. 8.

Fig. 9 is a bone knife or scraper very rudely made from a rib. Fig. 10 is a bone implement, much better fashioned, of the form of a chisel, though the edge is hardly sharp enough to have been used otherwise than as a scraper.

PLATE IV.

HAMMERS, PESTLES, OR MAULS.

FIG. 1. Broken oval beach stone used as a hammer.
From Midden.
$\frac{1}{3}$ actual size.

FIG. 2. Beach stone used at smaller end as hammer.
From Kist No. 7.
$\frac{1}{3}$ actual size.

FIG. 3. Stone hammer used at both ends.
From Kist No. 9.
$\frac{1}{3}$ actual size.

FIGS. 4–7. Stone hammers from Middens.
$\frac{1}{3}$ actual size.

FIG. 8. Stone maul worn at smaller end.
From Harbour Midden.
$\frac{1}{4}$ actual size.

These stone hammers or pounders are the most common and characteristic implements of the North British Kjökkenmöddings. They are found in all those which I have examined even cursorily in Caithness and Orkney, though I am not aware that they have been previously noticed in kists. They are mostly smooth beach stones, evidently used without a handle; but fig. 6 shows a rude commencement of a circular groove or depression for attachment to a handle, and fig. 7 shows some approximation towards the form of the ordinary celt.

It is remarkable that with this exception there is hardly a single one among the numerous stone relics which shows the least approach to the form of the polished stone celt, which at a later period became the most common tool or weapon used by the living and buried with the dead.

Fig. 8 is a ponderous block of rather soft sandstone of different and more regular form than any of the others. I conjecture it to have been a maul, used in battle, or for felling large animals, as it would have been a deadly weapon for such purposes, while it is not hard enough to have been used for pounding in a stone mortar. It seems to have been fashioned at the base for the reception of a round pole as a handle, in which respect it shows a marked advance; but it must be recollected that it came from the Harbour Midden, where there had been successive occupation, and I cannot be quite certain that it is of the same period as the ruder implements. Connected with these stone hammers or pounders are the stone mortars, which are simply solid blocks of stone with a rudely formed cavity or depression on one side. None of them were circular enough to have been used as querns; some may have been used as lamps or to hold water; but on the whole they have more the appearance of being simply mortars, in which bones or possibly grain were pounded by the hand hammers.

PLATE V.

HEFTS OR HANDLES.

FIG. 1. Heft or handle of bone.
From Harbour Midden.
½ actual size.

FIG. 2. Small deer's horn hollowed out as a handle.
From Churchyard Midden.
½ actual size.

FIG. 3-7. Hefts or sockets of bone. From Middens.
½ actual size.

FIG. 8. Deer's horn handle with small quartz chisel or scraper. From Kist No. 9.
½ actual size.

PLATE VI.

PINS, BODKINS, OR SKEWERS.

FIGS. 1-8. Pins, bodkins, or skewers of bone.
From Middens.
½ actual size.

FIG. 9. Well finished bone pin from Upper Midden.
½ actual size.

Figs. 1-6 illustrate the rudest forms, which are very common, consisting of mere chips or fragments of bone worked roughly to a point at one end.

Figs. 7 and 8 show more careful construction, being cut into something like shape with rude heads. Fig. 7 is a common form. Fig. 8 is unique and curious from its rude resemblance to a large iron nail.

Fig. 9 from the Upper Harbour Midden of the later occupants, illustrates the great progress which had been made from the first rude implements.

PLATE VII.

MISCELLANEOUS.

FIGS. 1–3. Whorls of stone, from Middens.
½ actual size.
FIGS. 4–6. Whorls of bone, from Middens.
½ actual size.
FIG. 7. Thin piece of bone cut into the form of a triangle. From Harbour Midden.
½ actual size.
FIG. 8. Broken circular stone plate, showing indentation on opposite sides. From outside of Chief's Kist.
½ actual size.
FIG. 9. Stone block with circular indentation on opposite sides. From outside of Chief's Kist.
⅙ actual size.

Fig. 7 is cut very exactly into the form of an equilateral triangle. I never saw anything like it, and conjecture it to have been a charm or amulet. It was from the upper half of the Harbour Midden, and may have belonged to the later occupants.

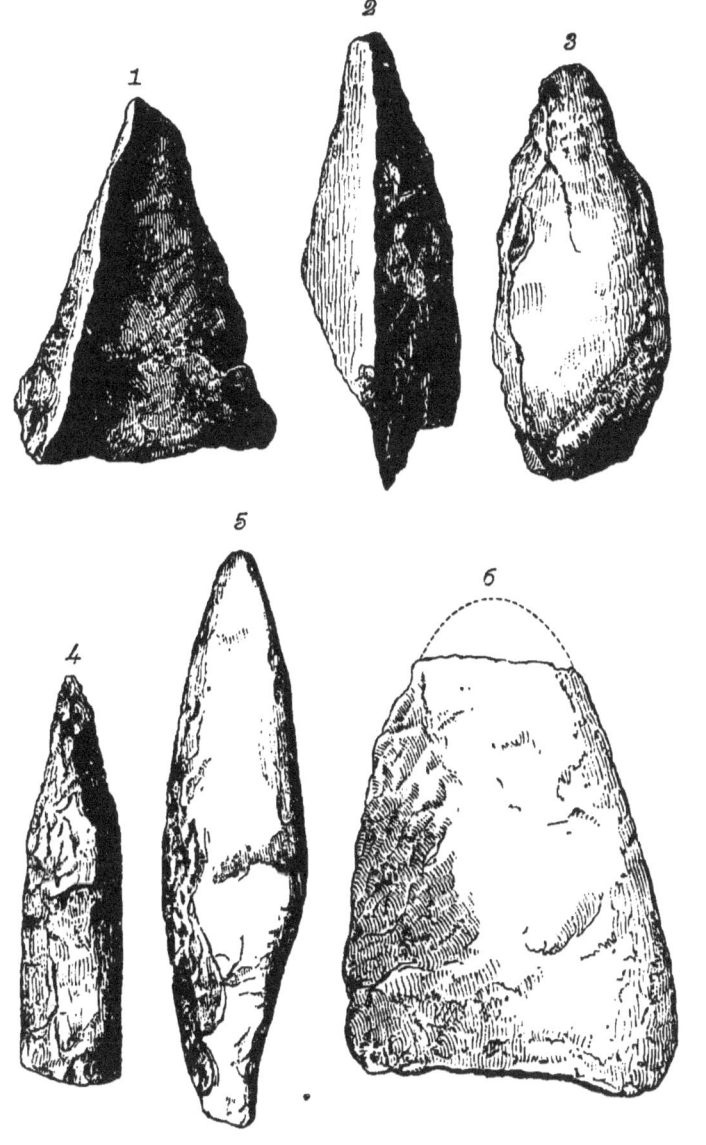

PLATE I.

Battle Axe and Spear-heads.

Arrow-heads. PLATE II.

PLATE III.

Knives, Scrapers, or Chisels.

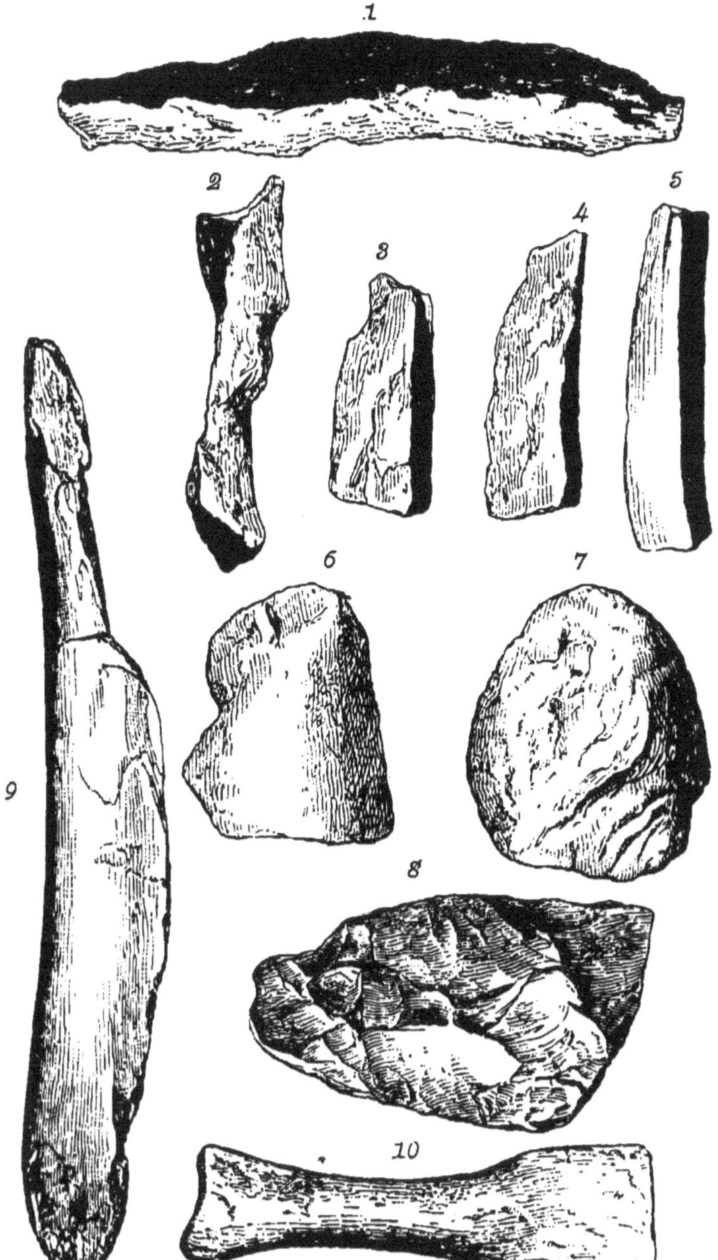

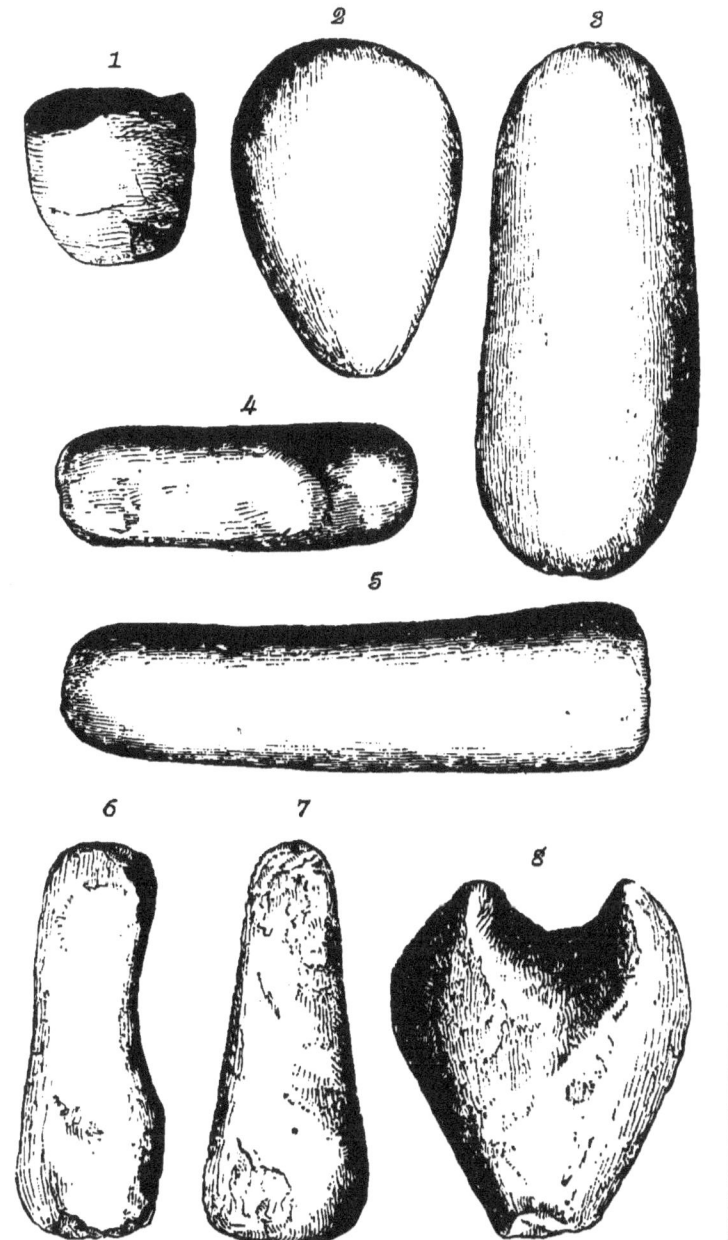

PLATE IV.
Hammers, Pestles, or Mauls.

PLATE V.

Hefts or Handles.

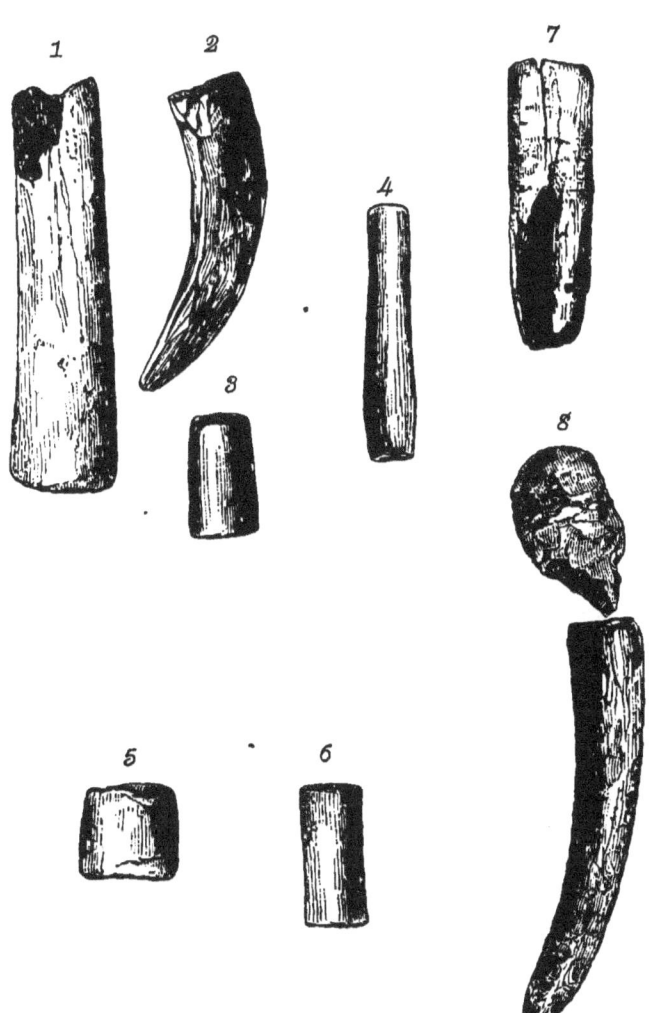

PLATE VI.

Pins, Bodkins, or Skewers.

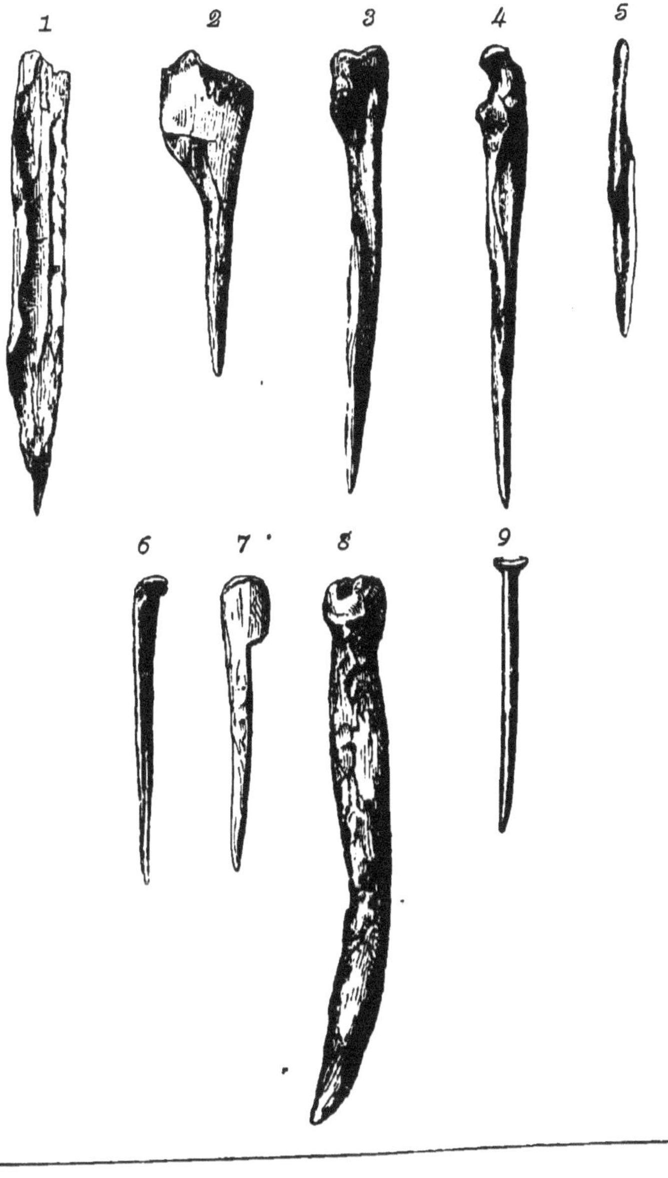

1 2 3 4 5

6 7 8 9

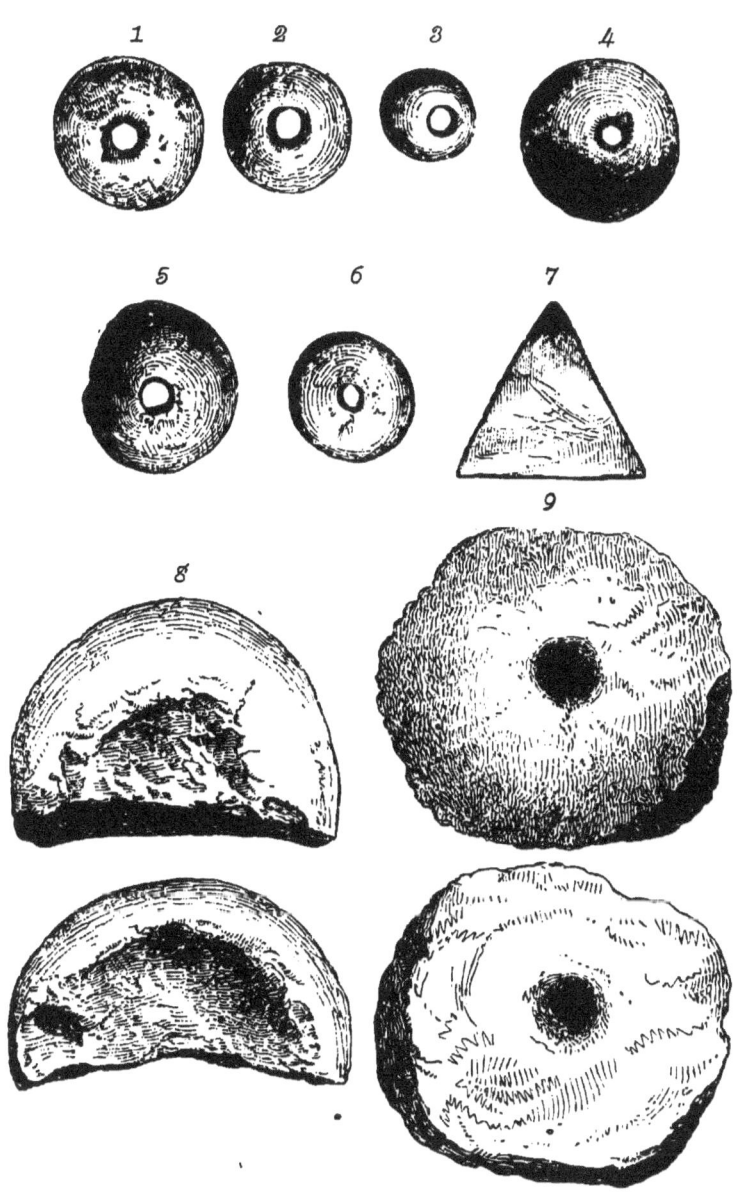

NOTES

UPON THE HUMAN REMAINS,

BY

THOMAS H. HUXLEY, F.R.S.

NOTES
UPON THE
HUMAN REMAINS FROM KEISS.
BY
THOMAS H. HUXLEY, F.R.S.

THE human remains from Keiss submitted to me by Mr. Laing consist of the greater part of one skeleton with many portions of others; and comprise nine skulls and fragments of skulls, with four more or less complete pelves belonging to certain of the skulls, besides bones of the limbs and of other regions of the body.

What I have to say respecting them will be arranged under the following heads:

I. A description of the human remains from Keiss.

II. A comparison of these remains with one another and a discussion of their ethnological characters.

In describing the crania I shall adopt, in principle, and mainly, in detail, the convenient nomenclature which has been gradually developed by Retzius, Broca, Welcker, and Thurnam, and which is employed by the latter writer in his valuable essay "On the Principal Forms of Ancient British and Gaulish Skulls." The term *cephalic index*, in this nomenclature, indicates the ratio of the extreme transverse to the extreme longitudinal diameter of a skull, the latter measurement being taken as unity. Skulls with a cephalic index of 0.8, or more, are *Brachycephalic*,* or "round." Those

* "Brachycephalic" is of course in strictness applicable to the people to whom the skulls belong; but custom has sanctioned the looser use of the word.

with the cephalic index less than 0.8 are *Dolichocephalic*. It is in this sense that the terms dolichocephalic and brachycephalic were used by their inventor Retzius, so far as he defined them at all:

"Vous me demandez les caractères distinctifs entre la forme brachycéphale et dolichocéphale! Je ne veux pas encore determiner quelques mesures fixes pour les distinguer; mais, à l'ordinaire, le diamètre longitudinal des dolichocéphales surpasse la largeur d'environ $\frac{1}{4}$, tandis que chez les brachycéphales cette difference varie entre $\frac{1}{5} - \frac{1}{8}$." ("Ethnologische Schriften," p. 118).

As Retzius considers the Swedish skulls with an index of .773 (*l.c.* page 4) to be eminently dolichocephalic, he must mean by the above expression, that, in a dolichocephalic skull, the long diameter exceeds the short by at least a fourth of that short diameter. In other words that the length is, at least, as 1000 : 800. If he had meant that the long diameter exceeds the short only by one-fourth of the long diameter, no skull would have been dolichocephalic unless the long diameter had to the short the proportion of 1000 : 750, a definition which would exclude his Swedish skulls from the dolichocephalic group. For this reason I must dissent from the interpretation which the editor of Retzius' Ethnologische Schriften puts upon his author's words (*l.c.* page 121, note). But apart from any question as to what may have been Retzius' meaning, the terms brachycephalic and dolichocephalic have been so extensively used, in this country and elsewhere, to denote skulls with the cephalic index above and below 0.8 respectively, that great inconvenience would result from attaching any other signification to them.

While objecting, however, to the use of "dolichocephalic" in any new sense, I quite agree with Broca, Welcker and Thurnam in thinking it expedient to sub-divide the dolichocephalic division; and, in doing this, I shall adopt the very convenient grouping suggested by Dr. Thurnam, who arranges the cephalic indices below .80 into four groups:

I. II. III. IV.
(.79 .78 .77); (.76 .75 .74); (.73 .72 .71); (.70 and below).

To No. I. Dr. Thurnam gives the name *sub-brachycephalic* used by M. Broca, and which I shall adopt, though not without some reluctance, on account of its etymological hybridity.

No. II. is the *orthocephalic* division.

No. III. is called *subdolichocephalic*, and No. IV. *dolichocephalic*, by Dr. Thurnam; but I object to both names for the reasons given above, and I substitute for No. II. the title of *mecocephalic*, and for No. III. *mecistocephalic*. Finally, I propose to sub-divide the Brachycephali into *Eurycephali*, with the cephalic index .80 to .84, and *Brachistocephali*, with the cephalic index .85 and above. The following table will make this terminology plain, and exhibit its relations to that already in use:

Cephalic index,	at or above .80 =	I. BRACHYCEPHALI, round skulls.
,,	at or above .85 =	*Brachistocephali*,
,,	below .85 and at or above .80 =	*Eurycephali*.
Cephalic index,	below .80 = II.	DOLICHOCEPHALI, long skulls.
,,	below .80 and at or above .77 =	a. *Sub-brachycephali*, ⎫
,,	below .77 ,, .74 =	b. *Orthocephali*, ⎬ oval skulls.
,,	below .74 ,, .71 =	c. *Mecocephali*, ⎭
,,	below .71 =	d. *Mecistocephali*, oblong skulls.

I.—A DESCRIPTION OF THE HUMAN REMAINS FROM KEISS.

I now proceed to describe the six skulls from Keiss and the other bones associated with them, indicating each set by the numbers affixed to them by Mr. Laing.

1. *The Bones marked No. 7.*

The skull (figs. 1 to 5), though slightly damaged, is in a

very fair state of preservation, and is a remarkably well formed and spacious cranium. The cephalic index is 0.78, and it therefore belongs to the sub-brachycephalic division.

The nasal depression and the supraciliary prominences are moderate; the forehead is well arched, though not high, and rises almost vertically from the brows. The superior curved line is well developed, and the occipital spine is strong; but the broad and convex occiput projects beyond it, when the glabello-occipital line is made horizontal.

The coronal suture is traceable throughout; the sagittal and the middle part of the lambdoidal are almost completely obliterated. A flat, broad depression runs along the middle line of the skull, in the region of the posterior half of the sagittal suture (fig. 2).

The upper contour of the squamosal is nearly straight; the mastoid processes large and prominent; the nasal bones well developed and projecting. The upper jaw is massive, with a sharp and strongly marked *spina nasalis anterior*. But there is no prognathism and the outer surface of the alveolar region is almost perpendicular. The lower jaw has very massive horizontal and perpendicular branches, and the mental prominence is so well marked that, when the zygoma is horizontal, the chin projects as far as the level of the extremities of the nasal bones.

In the upper view (or *norma verticalis*) of the skull (fig. 2) its broad and rounded figure is well displayed, and it will be observed that no part of either the jaws or the zygomata is visible. The front view (*norma frontalis*) (fig. 3) exhibits the massiveness of the jaws, which yet in no wise predominate over the brain case. The upper jaw, in fact, is not so round and full in front as might be anticipated from the general mass of the facial region. The arch of the palate is consequently (fig. 5) particularly acute, and the fore part of the face looks, as it were, pinched. In accordance with this, the nasal bones are prominent, and meet at an acute angle, so as to form a dorsal ridge in the upper part of their extent. The back view (*norma occipitalis*) (fig. 4) shows the rounding off of the parietal and sagittal regions, so that the contour is more arched than pentagonal, and, furthermore, reveals a slight want of symmetry in the two sides. The palate (fig. 5) is remarkably deep and rather narrow, measuring 1.95 in. from the incisor alveolar margin to the level of the posterior boundary on each side; 1.5 in. opposite the two last molar teeth where it is broadest; and having a depth of 0.67 in. from the roof to the alveolar margin, where it is deepest, which is at a point close to the posterior edge.

The occipital foramen is directed downwards and forwards. The mastoid processes are large, the supra-auditory ridges strong, and the styloid processes are strong and well ossified. The left upper canine is thrust inwards out of its place, while in the lower jaw the teeth are regular. In both jaws, the enamel of the incisors and of the molars is worn away so as to expose the dentine, but there is no symptom of decay in any of the teeth.

The sacrum and three fragments of the left innominate bone belonging to the same skeleton as the skull No. 7 were obtained by Mr. Laing. When they were carefully put together, and the right innominate bone was restored after the model of the left, the result was the pelvis represented in figs. 6–8, which are reduced to one-fourth of the natural size. The transverse diameter of the brim of the pelvis is, as nearly as I can judge from measurement of the specimen, 4.6 in.—the figure making this diameter slightly too small. The oblique diameter is equal to the transverse. The promontory of the sacrum is broken away, whence the precise ascertainment of the antero-posterior diameter becomes impossible, but it cannot have exceeded 3.8 in. The sacrum is markedly concave forwards, the pubic angles acute, the descending rami of the pubis are straight and not arcuated, and the true pelvis is deep. In fact, this is a well marked male pelvis differing in no important respect from the ordinary pelvis of the European male, though it is rather smaller than the average. From the measurements of the sacrum and those of the acetabulum, I conceive that the stature of No. 7 must have been below, rather than above, the middle height, perhaps five feet four or five inches.

2. *The Bones marked No.* 8.

The skull is orthocephalic, the cephalic index being 0.76. The calvaria is remarkable for the projection of the supraciliary ridges, caused by the great development of the frontal sinuses, the prominences formed by which are separated by but a very slight median depression. The forehead is low, narrow and receding, and the median contour of the skull slopes from it, gradually upwards, towards the vertex. The occipital spine is very strong, curved, and prominent, and the cerebellar region below it, strongly convex downwards. The supra-auditory ridge and the mastoid processes are very strong, and the styloid processes seem to have been no less so.

The *norma verticalis* (fig. 10) shows that the skull is narrower in the frontal region and widens out towards the parietal tuberosities. The sagittal and lambdoidal sutures are open throughout; the coronal is open above, but is obliterated for about an inch and a half at each of its outer ends. There is a large Wormian bone in the right crus of the lambdoid suture. The *norma occipitalis* (fig. 12) shows that the transverse contour of the skull inclines to be pentagonal and wall-sided.

The facial bones of this skull were entirely detached, and, like the base of the skull, much broken. However, of the lower jaw rather more than the left half was entire; and of the face the left jugal, left maxilla, and part of the right maxilla were preserved. Consequently, by articulating the mandible, making its median line coincide with that of the skull, and then adjusting the teeth of the fragmentary upper jaw to those of the lower, and the jugal to the external orbital process of the frontal, it was possible to restore the left half of the face, as in fig. 9. The prognathism of the skull thus restored is remarkable, especially since the front walls of the alveoli, in the premaxillary region and in the front part of the lower jaw, are broken away; the front tooth shown in the figure, being the canine in the upper jaw, and the outer incisor in the lower.

The axis of the *foramen magnum*—that is, a line drawn perpendicularly to its plane and through its centre—of this skull is directed, not downwards and forwards, as in human skulls in general, but downwards and backwards.

The sacrum, though it consists of only the ordinary five vertebræ, is as long as it is broad, and has a well marked anterior concavity. The greater sacro-sciatic notch is not more open than usual; the true pelvis is deep, and all the ridges and tuberosities of the bones are well developed. The axes of the acetabula are directed well forwards as well as outwards (figs. 14, 15, 16).

The vertebral fragments consist of the neural arches and attached posterior segments of the bodies of the second and third lumbar vertebræ. The fragments are naturally adjusted, and the distance from the upper face of the body of the one to the lower face of the body of the next, under these circumstances, is 2.6 in., which gives a height of 1.3 in. for each vertebra. The spinous processes, transverse processes, metapophysial and anapophysial tubercles are all remarkably strong and well developed.

The other bones belonging to No. 8 are the greater part of each innominate bone, the right and left femora, and tibiæ, the two humeri, minus their proximal ends, and some fragments of the fibulæ and lumbar vertebræ. On carefully joining the sacrum with the fragmentary innominate bones, the result was the pelvis represented in figs. 14–16. As the pubis and the ascending ramus of the ischium of each side are wanting, all the measurements of the brim cannot be ascertained. Its transverse diameter, however, is 4.7 in., and from the direction of what is preserved of the lateral boundaries (fig. 16), I do not believe the conjugate diameter exceeded 4.0 in.

There is nothing worthy of special notice about the other bones, except that they are strong, and have all their processes and ridges well developed. The femur is 18.7 in. long, which, by computation, would give the stature at 5 ft. 8 in. But the tibiæ are only 14.7 in. long, or nearly an inch shorter than they should be, in proportion to the length of the thigh bone. This deficit may have been made up by an unusual length of the strong spine, but it is quite safe to assume sixty-eight inches as the maximum height which this individual can have possessed.

3. *The Bones marked No. 2.*

The skull is small, measuring only 6.9 in. in length by 5.4 in. in breadth. It belongs, consequently, to the subbrachycephalic group, the cephalic index being 0.78. The supraciliary ridges are but little developed, and though the nasal bones are absent, the space for their insertion extends so far as to show that the nasal depression must have been very slight and shallow. The contour of the forehead is somewhat receding, the occiput rounded and projecting beyond the occipital spine, which is but feebly marked, and below which the cerebellar regions are full and convex. The styloid and mastoid processes are not large, but the upper boundaries of the temporal fossæ are defined by well-marked ridges and grooves (fig. 17).

In the *norma verticalis* (fig. 18) the contour of the skull appears pretty evenly oval, and in the *norma frontalis* (fig. 19) and *occipitalis* (fig. 20) it is well rounded and free from angles.

Corresponding with the posterior half of the sagittal suture, there is a remarkable flattening of the vertex, which is hardly noticeable in the true profile view of the skull, but becomes very obvious when the skull is turned a little obliquely. The middle three-fifths of the sagittal suture are obliterated, but the coronal and lambdoidal sutures are open throughout. The axis of the occipital foramen looks downwards and a little forwards.

The facial region is relatively small, and the bones delicate. The upper jaw exhibits a distinctly marked alveolar prognathism; the palate is narrowed, and its arch somewhat acuminated in front (fig. 21). The lower jaw has a well developed mental prominence. The wisdom teeth have been cut, on both sides, in this jaw, but that on the left side, which is alone retained, is not much worn.

The other bones belonging to No. 2 are a complete pelvis, a right femur, tibia, and fibula, a left humerus, radius, and ulna. The length of the femur is 16.75 in.; the mutilated right tibia could not have been less than 14 in. long. The humerus is 12.5 in. long, the radius not more than 9.1 in. The stature of this individual, therefore, probably did not exceed 5 ft. or 5 ft. 1 in. Taking this circumstance, together with the slenderness of the bones and the general aspect of the skull, into consideration, I should be disposed to suspect the sex to be female, apart from the characters of the pelvis, which are in many ways remarkable and indeed anomalous.

The pelvis, in fact, is not more like that of the ordinary European female than it is like that of the ordinary European male (figs. 22–24). The bones composing it are light and slender. The sacrum consists of five vertebræ, and has a strongly marked anterior concavity. The ilia are as vertical as in an ordinary male pelvis. The axes of the acetabula are not more backwardly directed; the arch of the pubis does not exceed 60°, and the edges of the descending rami of the pubes are not widely arcuated. Further more, the depth of the true pelvis, from the iliopectineal eminence to the tuberosity of the ischium, is 3.9 in., which, though not so great as in a characteristic male pelvis, is considerably greater than in a characteristic female one. The distance between the inner faces of the tuberosities of the ischium is not more than 3.8 in., or more than is usual in the male, less than is usual in the female. In the ordinary European pelvis, both male and female, the transverse diameter of the brim usually greatly exceeds the conjugate, or antero-posterior, diameter. In this pelvis the conjugate diameter exceeds the transverse by about three-tenths of an inch, and amounts to fully 4.9 in. Again, the antero-posterior diameter of the cavity of the true pelvis is 6.4 in., which far exceeds any dimensions of an ordinary pelvis of either sex; and, in correspondence with this circumstance, the greater sacro-sciatic notch is exceedingly wide and open (fig. 23).

Notwithstanding the many male characters of this pelvis, I am led, partly, by its absolute spaciousness; partly, by the resemblance which it presents to the aberrant form of pelvis sometimes observed in the European female, and described by Weber as "wedge-shaped;" and, partly, by the features of the rest of the skeleton, to consider it as really that of a female. I may add, that though the pelvis is quite symmetrical, and exhibits no sign of distortion, there are exostoses upon the front faces of the two pubes near the symphysis, and upon the ilia and sacrum in the region of the synchondroses.

4. *The Bones marked No.* 1.

The bones marked No. 1 constitute the greater part of one skeleton, which is, in many respects, the most remarkable of all those obtained from Keiss.

The cranium (figs. 25-29) is mecocephalic, the cephalic index being as low as .73. The nasal depression is but slight, and the supraciliary prominences small. The longitudinal contour (fig. 25) of the long, low, and narrow calvaria passes from the prominent glabella upwards and backwards; and, from the frontal angulation, slopes still upwards and backwards to the vertex, which lies at about the middle of the length of the parietal bones. The occiput is rounded, and projects beyond the occipital spine, which, like the superior curved lines, is hardly at all developed. The cerebellar region, or *conceptaculum cerebelli*, is indicated by a strong convexity; the mastoid processes are small, and the supra-auditory ridges moderate; the styloid processes are long and strong.

The coronary, sagittal, and lambdoidal sutures are all open, and there is a marked median depression corresponding with the posterior half of the sagittal suture. The parietal foramina are inconspicuous. The axis of the occipital foramen looks downwards and forwards.

The face is not large in relation to the skull, but it is singularly prognathous, the inclination of the alveolar margin being very marked, and causing the upper incisor teeth to project beyond the lower ones. The angles of the lower jaw are rounded off, and the mental prominence projects strongly. The palate is elongated (fig. 29). The outer surfaces of the nasal bones meet at an acute angle, so as to give rise to a median ridge.

The *norma occipitalis* (fig. 28) shows the transverse contour of this skull to be nearly pentagonal.

The teeth are not larger than is usual among Europeans. The wisdom teeth are cut in both jaws; they are distinctly smaller than the other molars and are slightly worn.

The femora are 15.8 in. long, whence the stature should not exceed fifty-eight inches, or 4 ft. 10 in., a conclusion which is confirmed by the dimensions of other parts of the body. Thus, when the bones of the thigh, leg, and foot are adjusted together in their natural position, the whole length of the limb from the upper surface of the head of the femur to the under surface of the calcaneum is $30\frac{1}{2}$ inches. But the length of the leg measured in this way is always more than equal to the half height of the body, and in this case was probably from one to two inches less, which would bring us to the same stature as by the preceding computation. The limb bones are remarkable for the combination of strength and slenderness which they present.

The pelvis (figs. 31–33) is unfortunately incomplete in its symphysial region, but what there is of it is exceedingly interesting. The sacrum is broad, wider than it is long, and its anterior concavity is well marked. The ilia have broad, concave, and obliquely inclined upper surfaces.

The transverse diameter of the brim of the pelvis is 5.1 in. In consequence of the absence of the symphysis, and the broken state of the promontory of the sacrum, the conjugate diameter cannot be accurately ascertained, but it was certainly not less, while it probably was more, than 4.5 in. The subpubic arch has the characteristic width, rounded summit, and flanged out pubic boundaries observed in a well-formed European female. The distance from the ilio-pectineal eminence to the ischial tuberosity is only 3.6 in., which is rather less than the average depth in the well formed female European, so that the true pelvis has the characteristic female shallowness.

But this pelvis departs from the ordinary type of the well

formed European female in the great antero-posterior diameter of its cavity, which must have amounted to at least 5.3 in. while in the average European female this dimension does not exceed 4.8 in. In correspondence with this deviation from the ordinary type the sacro-sciatic notch is unusually wide.

There can be no doubt from the characters of the pelvis and from those of other parts of this skeleton, that it appertains to a female.

5. *The Bones marked No. 3.*

These bones consist of a very perfect and beautiful skull (figs. 34–38), a left femur, and a right humerus.

The skull is orthocephalic (.76) and is that of an adult but young person; as the last molar tooth has made its appearance only on the right side of the upper jaw, and the enamel is preserved on all the molars, though the edges of the incisors are worn flat.

The nasal depression is very slight, the glabella prominent, but the supraciliary ridges little developed. The forehead is well formed and high. There is a slight flattening of the calvaria in the posterior parietal region, which is not quite sufficiently indicated in fig. 34. The occiput above the superior curved line is protuberant; the occipital spine is but slightly developed, and the cerebellar region is convex. The axis of the occipital foramen looks downwards and forwards.

The mastoid and styloid processes are moderately developed. The supra-auditory and supra-temporal ridges are but little marked. The *spina nasalis anterior* is well developed, and the alveolar surface of the premaxillæ is nearly perpendicular. The coronal and sagittal sutures are becoming obliterated. The parietal foramina are remarkably conspicuous, and symmetrically disposed.

In the *norma occipitalis* (fig. 37) all the angles of the transverse contour are completely rounded off.

The mandible has a strong mental prominence, its angles are incurved, and the lower contour of the horizontal portion of each ramus is convex. The palate is well arched, and symmetrically proportioned. All the characters of this skull indicate that it belongs to a female under thirty years of age.

The left femur and the right humerus of this skeleton are preserved. The former is 16.75 in. long, which, if we reckon the length of the femur as .275 of the height, would give a stature of about 5 ft. 1 in. The humerus has a length of twelve inches, which is somewhat more than it should be in proportion to the femur. The bones are slender, but the *linea aspera* of the femur is sharp and prominent.

6. *The bones marked No. 5.*

No. 5 is represented only by a skull, which is a good deal damaged (figs. 39–43). The skull belongs to the orthocephalic division, its cephalic index being .75.

The nasal bones unite into a sharp longitudinal ridge. The nasal depression is slight; the supraciliary protuberances moderate; the glabella prominent. The forehead is well arched, and the contour of the skull rises as far as a point a little way behind the coronal suture. The upper part of the occipital squama is produced into a protuberance, which projects far beyond the superior curved line and the occipital spine, the latter being hardly distinguishable. The cerebellar region is very convex. The axis of the occipital foramen looks downwards and forwards. The mastoid processes are small, the supra-auditory and temporal ridges little marked.

The sagittal suture is completely obliterated; the coronal is obliterated at its outer ends.

The palate is long and narrow, and there is marked alveolar prognathism. The mental prominence of the lower jaw is well developed. The wisdom teeth seem all to have been cut, but that on the right side in the lower jaw, which is alone preserved, is hardly at all worn. The other teeth have their cutting and crushing surfaces ground flat.

The bony framework of this skull is remarkably thin and light; and its numerous fractures appear to arise, at any rate in part, from this circumstance.

The *norma occipitalis* (fig. 42) and *frontalis* (fig. 41) of the skull show its transverse contour to be much rounded. The *norma verticalis* (fig. 40) is remarkable for the elongate ovoid figure of the circumference, and for the inequality of the two sides. This appears more marked in the figure than it really is, from the circumstance that one-half of the most protuberant portion of the occiput is fractured, while the other is entire.

I entertain no doubt that the skull appertained to a female, probably under thirty years of age.

I am indebted to my friend, William Turner, M.B., Demonstrator of Anatomy in the University of Edinburgh, for the following very interesting account of some remains of a female skeleton from Keiss, in his possession, which I have not seen.

"The skull, pelvis, and thigh bones described below were given me some months ago by my friend Dr. Arthur Mitchell. They were found in a stone kist in the ancient burying place on the links of Keiss. The kist was in the same line of graves from which Mr. Laing obtained a female skull in the course of his excavations. The bones form part of a female skeleton, and are in a good state of preservation. The woman to whom they had belonged had apparently reached the middle period of life.

The cranium possesses an elongated oval form. The forehead is smooth and not receding, the supraciliary ridges and glabella are only faintly marked. The upper region of the frontal bone is somewhat roof-shaped, and the same character is displayed by the anterior part of the parietal region. Posteriorly, the parietal bones curve gradually, backwards and downwards, to the lambdoidal suture, below which the upper squama of the occiput bulges backward in a very decided manner. The occipital muscular ridges and protuberance are faintly marked. The cerebellar fossæ are well seen. The sides of the skull are rather flattened. The cranial sutures are all marked externally.

The nasal bones are aquiline in form. The face is narrow, especially in the region of the upper jaw, and there is no prognathism. The teeth are much worn down on the surfaces of the crowns, which are flattened, and the dentine is exposed, but there is no decay. This condition of the teeth I have seen, not only in crania found in the more ancient graves, but in those obtained from mediæval tombs. The angle of the lower jaw is gently rounded, and the symphysis is somewhat pointed.

The bones of the cranium and face exhibit that general delicacy of structure and absence of strong ridges and processes which are so characteristic of the female skull. In its general proportions the cranium is strongly dolichocephalic, the bulging of the occipital squama contributing materially to its length. The cranial capacity, taken with fine sand, is 89 cubic inches, which places the brain-case quite on a par with, if not somewhat in excess of, the average cranial capacity of the women of our island at the present day.

The relative proportions of the different regions of the skull may be gathered from the following measurements :*—

* Most of the measurements are taken after the method of Mr. Busk. In estimating the maxillary radius the line is drawn to the most projecting part of

Extreme length, 7.2 in.; breadth, 5.1; height, 5.2.
Greatest frontal breadth, 4.3; parietal, 5.0; occipital, 4.3; zygomatic, 4.75.
Maxillary radius, 3.7; fronto-nasal, 3.6; frontal, 4.3; vertical, 4.7; parietal, 4.85; occipital, 4.3.
Basi-cranial length, 3.7. Horizontal circumference, 20.3.
Longitudinal frontal arc, 4.8; parietal, 5.0; occipital, 4.9; sum, 14.7.
Frontal transverse arc, 11.6; vertical, 12.0; parietal, 13.2; occipital, 10.6.
Proportion of length to breadth, 70; height, 72; occipital radius, 59; maxillary radius, 51.
Lower jaw:—Distance between rami, 3.8 in.; depth at symphysis 1.0; from symphysis to angle, 3.4.

The pelvis, from the delicacy of the bones, the expanded iliac fossæ, the rounded form of the pubic arch, the size of the outlet and inlet, and the roomy cavity, is undoubtedly that of a female. The coccyx and last sacral vertebra, with one antero-superior iliac spine are broken off; in other respects it is complete. Its chief dimensions are as follows:—

Diameters:—*Of the brim*—Transverse, 4.5 in.; left oblique, 4.6; right oblique, 4.9; conjugate, 4.4. *Of the outlet*—Between ischial tubera, 4.6; between ischial spines, 4.3.

Between most projecting parts of iliac crests, 9.4.

Between sacro-iliac joints, 4.0.

Depth of true pelvis—At symphysis, 1.2; from pectineal eminence to ischial tuber, 3.8.

Depth of whole pelvis—Between iliac crest and ischial tuber, 7.0; between antero-superior spine and ischial tuber, 6.0.

the alveolar arch, teeth not included; similarly, in estimating the depth at the symphysis the teeth are not included. The basi-cranial line is from the anterior margin of the *foramen magnum* to the fronto-nasal suture.

In comparing the various diameters of this pelvis with each other, and with the dimensions of the average female pelvis, certain points of interest may be noted; the diameters of the inlet, for instance, are considerably below, whilst the transverse diameter of the outlet, at the tubera, is in excess of, the average; the increased breadth at the latter spot being due to the well marked eversion of the tuberosities. The transverse diameter at the brim is much below the average, and almost exactly corresponds with the antero-posterior. The difference between the oblique diameters on the right and left sides is due to a want of symmetry in the form of the two innominate bones, which imparts an oblique character to the entire pelvis.

The two thigh bones are slender and well formed; neither they nor the pelvic bones have the muscular ridges strongly developed. Their extreme length is seventeen inches. Calculating the height of the skeleton from the length of the thigh bone, one might place it at 5 ft. 4 in."

II.—A COMPARISON OF THE HUMAN REMAINS FROM KEISS WITH ONE ANOTHER AND A DISCUSSION OF THEIR PECULIARITIES.

A.—The Crania.

The remains which have been described appertain to seven individuals; of whom two are male and five are female.

Of the males:

Cephalic index.
No. 7 is (?) in. high; is sub-brachycephalic (0.78) and has an ordinary pelvis.
No. 8 is 67-8 in. high; is orthocephalic (0.76) and has an ordinary pelvis.

mean 0.77 (or sub-brachycephalic).

Of the females:

Cephalic index.

No. 2 is 61 in. high; is sub-brachycephalic (0.78) and has an aberrant pelvis.
No. 1 is 58-9 in. high; is mecocephalic (0.73) and has a pelvis of less remarkable character, though slightly modified in the same direction.
No. 3 is 61 in. high; is orthocephalic (0.76) and no pelvis is preserved.
No. 5 is (?) in. high; is orthocephalic (0.75) and is devoid of pelvis.
No. 9* is 61-2 in. high; is mecistocephalic (0.70) has a pelvis nearly resembling that of No. 2.

mean 0.744 (or orthocephalic.)

Thus the males are, the one somewhat above and the other probably about, the average stature; while the females are short, none exceeding five feet two or three inches in height.

The males are, in the mean, shorter headed than the females, in accordance with the usual rule.

The males both have ordinary pelves; while it is a most remarkable circumstance that all the female pelves which are preserved differ from the ordinary female pelvis, in the circumstances that the conjugate diameter of the brim or the antero-posterior diameter of the cavity, or both, are unusually great. In two of the three this aberration goes so far, that the conjugate diameter nearly equals, or even exceeds, the transverse. In the recent state, the transverse diameters were, doubtless, somewhat greater than they appear to be in pelves put together without their synchondrosial cartilages and interpubic ligaments; but when due allowance is made for this circumstance, the differences between these and the ordinary female pelvis remain but little diminished.

None of the skulls exhibit paramastoid or pneumatic processes of the occipital bone; in none does the squamosal meet the frontal, so as to exclude the parietal from junction with the alisphenoid. None exhibit a persistent infraorbital

---

* That described by Mr. Turner. I should estimate the stature of this individual at an inch or two less than he does.

suture, or a second lachrymal; or that separation of the lachrymal from the *os planum* of the ethmoid by the junction of the frontal with the maxillary, which I have met with in some rare cases in the human skull, and which is a curious pithecoid variation, observed in the gorilla and the chimpanzee, but not in the orang. In all, the occiput forms a distinct projection above the superior curved line and *spina occipitalis*. There is no excessive development of the supraciliary ridges. Only the faintest traces of the premaxillomaxillary suture are to be seen in any of the skulls.

Taking the seven skulls as a whole, it will be observed that three are orthocephalic; two are sub-brachycephalic; one is mecocephalic; and one mecistocephalic. None of the skulls come within the proper brachycephalic group. Nevertheless there are very marked and obvious differences between No. 7 and Nos. 1 and 9.

The two male skulls Nos. 7 and 8 offer clear differences, which are even more apparent when the skulls themselves are placed side by side, than they seem to be in the figures. Of the five female skulls, Nos. 2 and 3 present resemblances to the male skulls; but Nos. 5 and 1 differ widely both from one another and from the male skulls. From some camera lucida sketches of No. 9, with which Mr. Turner has kindly favoured me, I judge that No. 9 resembled No. 1 more than any other skull in the collection.

Four forms—two male and two female—are distinguishable in this small collection of crania from Keiss.

Firstly. That characterised by its spacious and broad calvaria, with moderate nasal depression, wide and well-developed forehead, somewhat flat occiput, macrognathous and orthognathous face (No. 7).

Secondly. That characterised by a calvaria narrower in proportion to its length, especially in the frontal region, with a strong nasal depression, a narrower and more retreating forehead, a very prominent occipital protuberance or *probole*, well marked parietal protuberances, and a macrognathous and more prognathous face (No. 8).

Thirdly. That characterised by a long narrow calvaria, with a pentagonal contour of the *norma occipitalis*, with a slight nasal depression, a low and retreating forehead, a moderately prominent occiput, and with jaws which, though not large, are exceedingly prognathous (No. 1).

Fourthly. That characterised by an elongated oval thin calvaria, with a rounded contour of the *norma occipitalis*, with a slight nasal depression, moderately well formed forehead, prominent occiput, ill-marked parietal protuberances, and small and but slightly prognathous jaws (No. 5).

So much for the relations of these skulls to one another. Before I can make their affinities with other forms of European crania apparent, I must attempt to sum up, briefly, the results of the researches which, of late years, have been made into the cranial characters of the ancient and present inhabitants of central and north-western Europe.

In 1864 the Swiss naturalists, Professors Rütimeyer and His, published their important work entitled " Crania Helvetica," which embodies the results of their extensive investigations into the cranial characters of the present and former population of Switzerland, as determined by the skulls contained in ancient and modern burying-places and bone-houses. The work of these learned inquirers has an especial value, from the circumstance that they conducted their investigations and classified their materials as naturalists; and only when they had arrived, in this way, at a definite classification of the crania, inquired how far their zoological combinations and separations tallied with the data furnished by history and archæology.

Working in this fashion, Messrs. Rütimeyer and His

found it necessary to distinguish, among the skulls of the ancient and modern Swiss, four typical forms, which they named after the localities in which they severally predominated, or were first met with. These types are—Firstly, the Disentis type; secondly, the Sion type; thirdly, the Hohberg type; fourthly, the Belair type.* Of these four types, the Disentis type is brachistocephalic, the average cephalic index of the skulls examined being .865; the Sion type is sub-brachycephalic, with the average cephalic index .772; the Hohberg type is mecistocephalic, the average cephalic index being .707; while the Belair type is orthocephalic, and has the cephalic index .758. The cephalic index of the Disentis skull varies between .975 and .818; that of the Sion type between .819 and .730; that of the Hohberg type between .729 and .678; and that of the Belair type between .762 and .728.

Besides this range of variation within the limits of each type, Rütimeyer and His recognise many transitional forms between the several types, which they term "Sion-Disentis," "Hohberg-Sion," etc.

The *Disentis* skull is short and broad, with the occiput flattened and set almost at a right angle to the vertex and base. The forehead is, for the most part, tolerably broad and high, the face generally orthognathous. The supraciliary ridges are moderately, or little, developed. There is reason to think that skulls of the Disentis type date back to pre-Roman and perhaps to still earlier periods.† However this may be, it is the predominant modern type; three-fourths of the people of Switzerland having such skulls at the present day.

---

* I have not enumerated these types in the same order as that adopted by Messrs. Rütimeyer and His.
† Rütimeyer and His, *l. cit.* p. 42.

The *Sion* cranium is characterised by the considerable development of the occiput backwards, as well as in breadth and height; by the strength of the supraciliary arches and the deep nasal depression; with the smooth rounding of all the contours of the skull. The face is orthognathous, and the nose broad at the base as compared with the Disentis type.

This form predominates among the skulls of pre-Roman age in Switzerland; while, at the present day, though it has not altogether diappeared, its occurrence is very scanty. The relative proportions of this and the Disentis type, in ancient times, are therefore the reverse of those which they bear to one another at present.

The *Hohberg* type is marked by the length and narrowness of the skull; the diminished prominence of the parietal protuberances; the facet-like manner in which the occipital protuberance projects; the excess of the height over the breadth of the skull and the occurrence of a sharp sagittal ridge along the vertex. The face is orthognathous.

Skulls of this type, older than the Roman epoch, have not been met with. They are to be found, but not abundantly, among the present population of Switzerland.

In the *Belair* type the skull is long, with small absolute height and flattened vertex; the contour of the forehead and of the occiput make an angle with that of the vertex; the supraciliary arches are hardly at all developed; and the dorsum of the nose is almost vertical; the face is moderately orthognathous.

Only half a dozen of these skulls, from graves of the Burgundian epoch, are described.

South-western Germany is conterminous with the northern frontiers of Switzerland, and it therefore becomes exceedingly interesting to compare the conclusions of the Swiss naturalists with the investigations of Professor Ecker as detailed in his "Crania Germaniæ meridionalis occidentalis," a description of the crania of the ancient and modern inhabitants of South-western Germany, published between 1863 and the present year.

In general, Professor Ecker's results agree in a remarkable manner with those of Rütimeyer and His, as to the facts of the case. Marked brachycephaly predominates among the modern inhabitants of this part of Germany; and to such a degree, that the average cephalic index of two hundred of their skulls was as great as .835. With some minor differences, the skulls of the modern Swabians, Bavarians, and Wurtemburgers are formed upon the Disentis type, and resemble those of the modern Swiss.

But skulls of this form occur only rarely and isolatedly, in the ancient burying-places of south-west Germany, and are especially infrequent in those of the kind called *Reihengräber*. The German archæologists, in fact, distinguish two kinds of ancient burying-places, one called *Hügel-gräber*, "grave-mounds;" and one termed *Reihen-gräber*, "grave-rows," in which last the graves are arranged, side by side, in long series, the feet of the corpse being commonly turned towards the east. Each skeleton is usually buried either in a sarcophagus formed of rough slabs of stone, or in a coffin consisting of a split trunk of a tree, the two halves of which have been hollowed out with axes, and so converted into a sort of rude box for the body. The dates of these burying-places appear to range, on the one hand, not earlier than the period of the Roman rule in these parts, and, on the other hand, as late as the eighth century. The "grave-rows" are more modern than the "grave-mounds," and good reasons are given for ascribing them to the Franks and Alemanni of the Merovingian period, between the fifth and sixth centuries A.D. The associated weapons are, in the main, of iron.

The *Grave-row skulls*, though mecocephalic, are almost mecistocephalic, the mean cephalic index not rising above .713, while the maxima and minima are .784 and .666. The brow is narrow and often low, and the supraciliary ridges generally strongly developed in male skulls, in which case there is a deep nasal depression. The *norma occipitalis* of the skull may be flatly arched, or gable-like and pentagonal above, the latter being usually the case in male skulls. Their most characteristic feature is the strong development of the upper part of the occipital squama, which projects, and is usually marked off from the vertex by a depression in the region of the smaller fontanelle.

Professor Ecker justly identifies these "grave-row" skulls, in general, with the Hohberg forms of Rütimeyer and His; and he considers the Belair type to be no distinct form, but simply one of the female modifications of this type. Among two hundred modern skulls of north-west Germany only one even approximated to this form, so that it may now be considered to be practically extinct in that part of Europe; but Professor Ecker demonstrates that the type of skull predominant among the present Swedes is identical with it.

On the other hand, in the old grave-rows, this type predominates, to the exclusion of the modern form of south-west German cranium. In the grave-mounds, which it will be remembered are older than the grave-rows, on the contrary, the crania do not exactly resemble either the grave-row, or the modern, type, but present a form transitional between the two. The grave-mound skulls have a mean cephalic index of .788; the maxima and minima being .752 and .829. The *norma occipitalis* is not pentagonal, and the occiput is evenly rounded.

I am not acquainted with any investigations into the cranial characters of the North Germans made with the same care and detail as those of Professor Ecker, except those of Professor Welcker, of Halle,* who has given the measurements of thirty male skulls. It is important to note that Halle is separated from South-western Germany by the central European high lands and the region of the old Hercynian forest. And though it is neither certain nor probable that all the skulls measured by Welcker proceeded from Halle and its neighbourhood, it is very likely that a large proportion did so, and therefore belonged to the basin of the Elbe and Weser, and not, like Ecker's crania, to that of the Rhine and Meuse.

The average cephalic index of all these "Halle" skulls is .805. Twelve are dolichocephalic, or range between .74 and .80; eighteen are brachycephalic, or between .80 and .88. None are mecistocephalic or mecocephalic, and only five belong to the orthocephalic division; thirteen are below .85 (eurycephali), and five range above it (brachistocephali). Clearly, therefore, as Welcker was the first to point out (thereby reversing the dictum of Retzius) the Halle Germans are a brachycephalic and not a dolichocephalic people. But it is no less important to observe, that though absolutely broad-headed, they are long-headed relatively to their south-western countrymen. For we have seen that in a hundred skulls of the latter people the mean cephalic index is .835; and none fall into the mecistocephalic, mecocephalic, or orthocephalic division; only fifteen are even sub-brachycephalic; while thirty-six are brachistocephalic, the cephalic index rising to .85 or more. Thus, taking per-centages, there are twice as many skulls with the cephalic index above .85 in South Germany as in Halle, while there are between two and three times as many dolichocephali in Halle as in South Germany.

* Untersuchungen über Wachsthum und Bau des Menschlichen Schädels.

With respect to the ancient population of this part of Germany very few data have fallen into my hands, or exist, so far as I know.

Dr. Adolph Friederich,* however, has figured and described seven crania, forming a part of a collection of human skeletons, forty-six in number altogether, discovered in course of levelling an ancient tumulus (" Altgermanische Tödtenhugel,"—apparently a Grave-row) at the village of Minsleben, near Wernigerode, in Prussian Saxony, at no very great distance from Halle; like it lying in the drainage area of the Elbe and adjacent rivers, and separated from the Rhine by the forests and mountains of central Germany. The skeletons, with one exception, lay with their skulls to the west and their feet to the east. In the same mound as that, in and about which, these skeletons were found, lay urns, covered with flat stones and containing burnt bones. But the urns were not inclosed in a stone chamber, and in this respect were like the urns found a quarter of a league further to the east, each of which had a flat, inverted, saucer-like cover. The mound contained urns and fragments of urns of variously formed and ornamented patterns; with many flint knives and flint arrow-heads. Only in two cases, one the body of a child and the other that of an adult, were rusty iron knives, lying on the left side of the thorax, discovered. Of animal bones, only a horse's skull with its upper cervical vertebræ at the feet of a man, and an ornamented horse's lower jaw, were found. Many large fire-places were met with at the bottom of the mound.

The largest skeleton measured 5 ft. 9 in. in height; the middle size, 5 ft.

* In a work entitled "Crania Germanica Hartagowensia, Beschreibung und Abbildung Altdeutscher Schädel aus einem Todtenhügel bei Minsleben in der Grafschaft Wernigerode," 1865.

On measuring the figures of these skulls, I find their cephalic indices to be as follows :—

	Length.	Breadth.	Cephalic index.	
No. II.	7.2	4.9	.68	} mecistocephalic.
I.	7.25	5.05	.69	
III.	7.75	5.5	.71	} mecocephalic.
VI.	7.1	5.15	.72	
IV.	7.30	5.45	.74	} orthocephalic.
VII.	6.8	5.15	.75	
V.	7.25	5.65	.77	sub-brachycephalic.

mean = .72

Thus these skulls all belong to the dolichocephalic division and the mean measurement of the seven would even place them in the mecocephalic group.

Dr. Friederich justly remarks upon the resemblance of some of these skulls to the Sion and Hohberg types of His and Rütimeyer. They are, in fact, strikingly like these and the Grave-row skulls of Ecker, but are more prognathous. This prognathism reaches its extreme in No. III.

Proceeding still further northward, the modern Danes, Swedes, and Norwegians are remarkable for the length of their skulls, and the very general development of an occipital tuber, or *probole*. Professor Ecker further points out that the Grave-row skulls of South Germany (and consequently the Hohberg forms of Rütimeyer and His) completely belong to the Scandinavian type; and he figures, not only modern Swedish skulls, but some ancient ones, which with the figures and descriptions given in the recently published collection of Retzius, "Ethnologische Schriften," fully bear out this conclusion. But since the investigations of Nilsson, Eschricht, and Retzius it has been known that some of the most ancient inhabitants of Denmark and Sweden possessed skulls of far broader form than those of the modern Scandinavians, whence has arisen the doctrine that the latter were preceded by a brachycephalic race.

Upon this point, Messrs. Davis and Thurnam have given very important information ("Crania Britannica," p. 246–7) by the help of which the precise value of the term "brachycephalic," as applied to the ancient Scandinavian skulls, may be tested.

In thirty-three male skulls from barrows, tumuli, and peat-mosses of Denmark and Sweden measured by these authors, the mean cephalic index does not rise above .78; and the average of thirteen female skulls is the same. The highest cephalic index, .85, is attained by only two skulls, one male and one female.

Of the thirty-three males, one is mecistocephalic, six are mecocephalic, four are orthocephalic, ten are sub-brachycephalic; so that there are twenty-one in the dolichocephalic division: while there are only twelve brachycephali; and, of these, but one reaches the limits of brachistocephaly. The cephalic index of an average modern Swedish skull is, according to Retzius ("Ethnologische Schriften," p. 4) .773. Unfortunately, he gives no series of measurements so as to enable one to classify the skulls in the fashion already adopted. Four Swedish skulls, the measurements of which are stated by Professor Ecker, have the indices .726, .722, .718, .695 = average, .715. Therefore, if Retzius is right in taking .773 as the average cephalic index, it would appear that a good many Swedish skulls must reach .80, in order to bring the average so high. It is more probable, however, that Retzius has assumed too high a mean index for the crania of his countrymen.

On considering the results obtained for the existing populations of Europe, from Switzerland to Scandinavia, we find:*

* The per-centages given must be regarded merely as approximatively correct.

1. That the Swiss are three-fourths brachycephalic; brachistocephaly being of frequent occurrence.

2. That of the South-west Germans, 85 per cent. are brachycephalic, 36 per cent. brachistocephalic, while only 15 per cent. are dolichocephalic.

3. That of the Halle Germans, a smaller proportion (60 per cent) are brachycephalic, and, of these, only 16 per cent. brachistocephalic, while the dolichocephali increase to 40 per cent.

4. That, among the modern Scandinavians, it is almost certain that none are brachistocephalic, and very few even brachycephalic; the great proportion being dolichocephali, and a large per-centage meco- and mecistocephali.

Thus, looking to the modern populations alone, there is every stage from brachistocephaly to mecistocephaly to be met with between Switzerland and Scandinavia—brachycephaly diminishing and dolichocephaly increasing with the latitude.

On the other hand,

1. The ancient Swiss, whose remains are preserved, were, at a certain epoch, almost wholly dolichocephali, with a small per centage of brachycephali.

2. The cephalic index of the ancient South-west Germans —Grave-mound and Grave-row skulls together—varied between .829 and .666 : the average of the two types being .75. They were, therefore, mainly dolichocephali, with a small per centage of brachycephali, and no brachistocephali.

3. The cephalic indices of the crania of the ancient North Germans of Minsleben vary between .77 and .68 and have a mean of .72. These people were, therefore, eminently dolichocephalic.

4. The ancient Scandinavians of Borreby, Moen, and other localities, have an average cephalic index of .78 ; the range

being between .85 and .72. Thirty-six per cent. are brachycephalic; but only one in a hundred is brachistocephalic.

Leaving the North Germans of Minsleben out of consideration for the present, on account of the small number of skulls examined, it appears that, at the epoch to which the skulls, here called "ancient," belonged, the extreme brachycephaly of the modern Swiss and South Germans was not to be met with in any of the localities hitherto examined; but that the most brachycephalic people were the Scandinavians, and the least so the ancient Swiss and Germans, thus, in a measure, reversing the existing order of things.

But it is to be carefully observed that the brachycephaly of ancient Scandinavia is a very different matter from that of modern Switzerland or South Germany; that, in fact, the ancient Scandinavians are far below even the Halle Germans (with 60 per cent. of brachycephaly) in this respect, and are but very little above the ancient South Germans, (if we combine both Grave-mound and Grave-row types,) while they are, as nearly as may be, equal to the Grave-mound type, the mean cephalic index of which is .788.

Thus, so far as our evidence goes, no ancient European people from Switzerland to Scandinavia was, as a whole, brachycephalic in the sense that the Halle Germans, still less in the sense that the Swiss and South Germans, are so. Brachycephaly amounting to 50 per cent. is a characteristic of modern populations in the localities, and within the period, now under discussion.

If, instead of taking a north and south line from Switzerland we attempt to follow an east and west one, and work out the craniology of France in the same way, we find that precise and detailed information concerning the cranial characters of the inhabitants of ancient and modern France is still a desideratum. The best data for ancient skulls are those furnished by Dr. Thurnam, who gives measurements of thirty-six, probably male, Gaulish skulls. Of these, nineteen are dolichocephali, seventeen brachycephali; and three of these last are brachistocephali. In other words, there is rather less than forty-eight per cent of brachycephaly, and nine per cent. of brachistocephaly. The average cephalic index is .78.

Among the ancient British and Irish skulls of which measurements are given by Drs. Davis and Thurnam, ninety-nine are English : of these, thirty-six are brachycephalic—twelve brachistocephalic. The average cephalic index is a little below .80.

Comparing the ancient Gaulish and British crania, as a whole, with those of other parts of Europe, they present much the same mixture of types as those from the tumuli of Denmark; and therefore I was not greatly surprised, though much pleased, when some time since Mr. Brown, of Burton-on-Trent, was so obliging as to send for my inspection the fragmentary cranium figured in the accompanying woodcuts (figs. 44–47).

This calvaria was found near Ledbury Hall, the seat of Lord Vernon, in Derbyshire. It was imbedded six to seven feet below the surface, in what seems to be an alluvial deposit formed by the river Dove, which runs at a short distance from the spot. Mr. Brown writes that "a very fine front of *Bos primigenius*, an equally characteristic one of *Bos longifrons*, horns of red deer, an oak tree, and other similar objects were disinterred in the course of the same works."

The calvaria has a brown colour as if it had lain in peat; but is otherwise but little different from a churchyard bone. It is 7.15 in. long, by 5.5 in. in greatest width ; its cephalic index, therefore, is .77. The supraciliary ridges are prominent and contain very large frontal sinuses, the walls of which are broken away in the region of the glabella. The middle part of the coronal suture, between the temporal ridges, is completely obliterated. The sagittal suture is, for the most part, obliterated. The parietal bones are raised up into a strong broad flattened ridge in about the middle of their length, in correspondence with the remarkable depth of the longitudinal sinus in this region. This peculiarity is not seen in fig. 47, owing to the position of the skull. The middle of the lambdoidal suture is obliterated. The superior curved line and occipital spine are very strong. The *squama occipitis* is particularly excavated, internally, so as to give ample room for the projection of the posterior lobes of the brain. The lateral sinus is distinct only on the right side, the longitudinal sinus seeming to pass completely into it on that side.

A little flattening and elongation, with a rather greater development of the supraciliary ridges, would convert this into the nearest likeness to the Neanderthal skull which has yet been discovered.*

Taking together the data furnished by Professor Wilson and by Drs. Davis and Thurnam, the measurements of thirty-six ancient Scotch skulls give twenty-four per cent. of brachycephaly; nine per cent. of brachistocephaly. The average cephalic index is only .760, being brought down by the large increase in the per centage of meco- and mecistocephalic skulls, which amount altogether to thirty-six per cent. In none of the previous groups does the per centage of these skulls rise to more than two-thirds that amount.

Mr. Turner has been so good as to supply me with the measurements of ten skulls from "long built-up stone cists, such as are not uncommon in various parts of Scotland. The cists were formed of slabs of stone, those constituting

* See Appendix *A*.

the ends and sides being placed on their edges, whilst the slabs which formed the roof and floor of the cist were laid flat and rested upon the upper edges of the end and side slabs. The skeletons found in these cists were laid out in the extended position. The cists were generally placed due east and west, and the skull was situated at the west end of the cist." The extreme cephalic indices of these skulls are .78 and .72; the mean, .741.

The mean cephalic index of thirty-three ancient Irish skulls, for measurements of which I am indebted to my friend Dr. E. P. Wright, Professor of Zoology in Trinity College, Dublin, is about .75. Calculating the per centages from this number, three would be mecistocephalic, twenty-four mecocephalic, fifteen orthocephalic, twenty-seven sub-brachycephalic, thirty brachycephalic; and of these last, six brachistocephalic. But it is right to add, that, of the two brachistocephalic skulls in the thirty-three, one is exceptional in possessing an open frontal suture, while its general features and its well-developed *probole* are quite in accordance with those of other ancient Irish skulls; the other is from a monasterial burying-ground, formerly occupying the site of St. John's Chapel, Dublin, and may be of foreign origin. The only remaining very broad skull (.84) in the series was obtained from the same burying-ground. Not one of the remaining skulls has a cephalic index exceeding .82.

Thirty-five Anglo-Saxon skulls measured by Messrs. Davis and Thurnam have a mean cephalic index of .750; with only nine per cent. of brachycephaly, and no brachistocephaly; while the mecisto- and mecocephalic skulls amount to thirty-nine per cent.

Thus it appears that none of the ancient inhabitants of

North-western Europe, whose remains have yet been examined, were, on the whole, nearly so brachycephalic as the Halle Germans of the present day; still less were they comparable, in this respect, to the Swiss, or the South-west Germans. Furthermore, brachycephaly, even in ancient times, seems, so far as the imperfect data allow us to judge, to have been more abundant in Switzerland and France, than in Scandinavia and England; in these last than in Scotland; and more abundant in Scotland than among the Anglo-Saxons, or the South Germans of the Grave-rows. In all these countries a long-headed people has existed, side by side with a broader headed one, for a longer or shorter period. In Scandinavia, Ireland, Scotland, England, the long-headed type has overcome the other, and predominates at the present day. In Germany and Switzerland, on the other hand, it is the broad head which has vanquished.

If we now look at the populations of Europe beyond the limits of the countries which have been named, all the evidence before us tends to show the existence, at all times, of an exclusively, or predominatingly, dolichocephalic population in the extreme west—in Ireland, in the Basque provinces, and in Spain; while in the extreme east, the Slavonic and Finnish populations, conterminous with the south and central Germans, are universally broad-headed. Dr. Thurnam well remarks: " I must confess that the correspondences between the skull form of the ancient brachycephalous Briton, Gaul, and Scandinavian, and that of the modern Finn, so very much exceed any differences which may be traced in them, that I should have no difficulty, on sufficient evidence, in admitting their common parentage and descent."

But this pregnant suggestion may be followed out much further. What Dr. Thurnam says of the skull of the Finn is no less true of the Swiss Disentis skull, the modern South German skull, and the Slavonian skull. The cranium of a

South Russian, figured in the "Bericht" of Von Baer and Wagner, is altogether of the same general type as the Disentis, or brachycephalic ancient Briton.

More than this. All these people, whether Finns, modern Swiss, South Germans, or Slavonians, are, in the main, a tall, fair, blue-eyed, and light-haired stock—*Xanthochroi*, as I have elsewhere termed them. The ancient inhabitants of Belgic Gaul, the Kimry of Thierry, were also a tall, blue-eyed and fair-haired people. As regards the nature of their skulls, W. Edwards and M. Broca assume, and the Baron de Belloguet has recently endeavoured to prove, that they were elongated; but the evidence he adduces would lead me to the contrary conclusion. His typical portrait of an ancient Gaul from the *æs grave* of Rimini would, with a little alteration of the chin, do very well for one of Ecker's Black-foresters, and the position of the ear with relation to the extreme hinder contour of the skull is such as to render it far more probable that the subject figured was short-headed than long-headed.*

But apart from the insufficiency of M. de Belloguet's evidence for the long-headedness of the Belgic Gauls, Dr. Thurnam's reasoning in favour of the contrary conclusion appears to me to be almost conclusive. For, in the first place, he shows that there is a broad distinction to be drawn between the crania found in the long barrows of Britain and those met with in the round barrows. In the latter, brachycephaly prevails, the mean cephalic index being .810—the maximum .870, and the brachycephaly amounting to sixty-six per cent. The average stature is at least 5 ft. 9 in.; two individuals reaching 5 ft. 11 in. and 6 ft. 2 in., respectively. Some of these crania closely resemble the Disentis and modern South

* Roget, Baron de Belloguet, "Ethnogénie Gauloise," 1861. M. de Belloguet strangely mixes up long faces with long skulls, as if a long face implied a long skull. For a further discussion on this subject, see Appendix *B*.

German forms; but, on the whole, they are probably nearer the Grave-mound and Borreby skulls.

And, in the next place, Dr. Thurnam brings forward strong reasons in favour of the opinion that these broad-headed, tall people of the round tumuli of Britain were the Belgæ of our islands and of continental Gaul. In this case they were certainly a fair and blue-eyed people of the same stock as those whom Thierry, rightly or wrongly, called "Kimry," and who entered very largely into the population of Gaul between the Seine and the Rhine. If this stock is represented, as I believe it to be, by the broad-headed folk who constituted a certain proportion of the populations of Switzerland, South-west Germany, and Scandinavia, in the most ancient times of which we have any archæological records—if, as I follow Dr. Thurnam in believing to be the case, no physical line of demarcation can be drawn between all these and the Finns: if further, as I believe, they are not more defined from the Slavonians, it follows that at one period or another, one great swarm of broad-headed Xanthochroi has extended across Europe from Britain to Sarmatia, and we know not how much further to the East and South.

Dr. Thurnam has further endeavoured to prove (and with much show of reason) that, in Britain, the broad-headed Belgæ were intruders upon more ancient dwellers in the land, who buried their dead in long barrows and had elongated crania. Whatever may be the truth as regards the relative antiquity of the two stocks, there can be no doubt respecting their physical differences. Dr. Thurnam figures a typical skull of these long-barrow Britons, which he thus describes (*l.c.* p. 25):

"The greatest length is 7.3 inches (the glabello-inial diameter 7.1 inches); the greatest breadth is 5.5 inches, being in the proportion of 75 to the length, taken as 100· The forehead is narrow and receding, and moderately high in the coronal region, behind which is a trace of a transverse depression. The parietal sutures are somewhat full, and add materially to the breadth of this otherwise narrow skull. The posterior borders of the parietals are prolonged backwards, to join a complex chain of Wormian bones in the line of the lambdoid suture. The superior scale of the occiput is full, rounded, and prominent; the inion more pronounced than usual in this class of dolichocephalic skulls. The supraciliaries are well marked, the orbits rather small and long; the nasals prominent; the facial bones short and small; the malars flat, and almost vertical; the alveolars short, but rather projecting; the mandible is comparatively small but angular; the chin square, narrow, and prominent."

The crania of the form just described appertain to a short race of people, not exceeding five feet six or seven inches in average height.

I can discern no differences of importance between these skulls from the long barrows and the crania (a typical example of which is represented in figs. 48–51) which I described, some years ago under the name of River-bed skulls, in a paper from which the following is an extract:*—

"The skull from Muskham, in the valley of the Trent, like the animal bones with which it was associated, is stained of a dark-brown colour. The whole of those parts of the cranial bones which bound the cranial cavity are well preserved; but the facial bones, with the exception of a small portion of the nasals, are broken away, so as to expose the whole of the under-surface of the base of the skull.

* "Notes upon Human Remains from the Valley of the Trent." — The Geologist, June, 1862. I have made two or three corrections and additions to the original.

"The considerable development of the frontal sinuses and of the different ridges and processes of the skull, shows it to be that of an adult, and the same characters lead me to believe that it belonged to a male. Otherwise it is small enough for a female, as its extreme length does not exceed 7.1 in., its extreme breadth 5.4 in.,* and its horizontal circumference 20½ inches.

"The skull has a very peculiar form. If a line drawn from the glabella to the superior curved line of the occiput be made horizontal, the highest point of the longitudinal median contour of the skull will be seen to be situated about the middle of the length of the sagittal suture; and, from this point the contour shelves rapidly downwards, to the brow on the one hand, and to the centre of the space between the apex of the lambdoidal suture and the occipital protuberance on the other. This last is the most prominent portion of the back part of the skull, the median contour below it bending forwards to the occipital spine, which is a very strong, projecting, triangular process. It follows from this description, that a line taken from the glabella to the occipital spine is shorter than one from the glabella to a point midway between this and the lambdoidal suture. The difference between the two is about 0.3 of an inch. I find that crania differ a good deal in this respect, the occipital spine being in many, especially the lower races of mankind, the most backwardly situated part of the skull, when the glabello-occipital line is made horizontal, while in others, as in the present instance, the most posterior part of the skull is situated much higher up.

"The line of greatest breadth of the skull is situated nearly in the same plane as that of its greatest height, in the position indicated, and the auditory foramina may also

* The cephalic index is, consequently, .76.

be said, roughly, to be intersected by that plane. The forehead is low and narrow, but not retreating. The supraciliary prominences are very well developed and, by their form, indicate the existence of large frontal sinuses. The space between the glabella and the nasal suture is not really very depressed, though on the side view of the skull it appears to be so, by reason of the projection of the supraorbital prominences.

"The vertical height of the skull, from the centre of the auditory foramen to the vertex, is 4.8 inches, and the centre of the auditory foramen lies about 0.8 of an inch below the level of the glabello-occipital line.

"The mastoid and styloid processes are well developed.

"The base of this skull is remarkable in several respects. The occipital foramen is placed far back, and its plane is directed more backwards than is usual in human skulls. When the base of the skull is turned upwards, and the glabello-occipital line is horizontal (its length being 6.7 inches), the anterior edge of the occipital foramen lies 1.5 inch above the line, and a perpendicular let fall from it would cut the line 3.9 inches from its anterior end. A similar line let fall from the posterior edge would cut the glabello-occipital line at 5.3 inches from its anterior end, and that edge is only 0.9 of an inch above it. In a length of 1.4, the plane of the occipital foramen, therefore, has a fall of 0.6 towards the glabello-occipital line.

"In a well-formed European skull, whose glabello-occipital line measures 7.0 inches, while its extreme length is 7.25, the distance of the anterior edge of the occipital foramen from the glabella, measured in the same way along the glabello-occipital line, is 3.8; of its posterior edge, 5.3. The anterior edge is 1.1 vertically above the line, and the posterior edge 1.0 above it. Thus, in a length of 1.5, the occipital foramen has a slope of only 0.1 inch, so that, instead of being greatly inclined backwards, it is nearly horizontal.

"The skull from the Valley of the Trent belongs to a cranial type which seems at one time to have been widely distributed over the British Islands. I have seen skulls from rude stone tombs in Scotland with similar characters, and others obtained from the Valley of the Thames. There are skulls in the Museum of the Royal College of Surgeons, exhibiting like proportions, from the remarkable tumulus at Towyn-y-Capel, Anglesea, described by the Hon. W. O. Stanley, M.P., in the 'Archæological Journal' (Institute) for 1846; and my friend, Mr. Busk, has shown me others from Cornwall. But the skulls which most closely resemble the Muskham cranium are some, also from river-beds, which I saw in the Museum of the Royal Irish Academy, and in the collection at Trinity College, Dublin, and of which my friend, Dr. E. P. Wright, the curator of that collection, has been good enough to supply me with excellent casts. Two of these skulls are from the bed of the Nore, in Queen's County, and two from that of the Blackwater river, in Armagh, and one of the latter has the most extraordinary resemblance to the Muskham skull, as the following table of measurements will show :—

	Muskham.	Blackwater.
Maximum length	7.0	7.25
Length of glabello-occipital line	6.7	7.0
Greatest vertical height from centre of auditory foramen, the glabello-occipital line being horizontal	4.8	4.7
Distance of auditory foramen below glabello-occipital line	0.8	0.7
Greatest transverse diameter	5.4	5.75
Transverse diameter at the lower ends of the coronal suture	4.4	4.75
Horizontal circumference	20.5	20.75
Transverse arc from one auditory foramen to the other	13.25	13.0
Anterio-posterior arc from glabella to occipital protuberance	12.5	12.5
Antero-posterior arc from glabella to posterior edge of the occipital foramen	14.25	14.4

"The edges of the occipital foramen of the Blackwater skull are broken, but its plane seems to be less inclined, so that this feature may be accidental in the Muskham skull. The frontal sinuses are less developed in the Blackwater skull, and it is broader, its cephalic index amounting to .79. The other Blackwater skull and one of the Nore skulls are also very like the Muskham skull, but the remaining Irish skull from the Nore is much larger (having a length of 8.0 inches) and more depressed. It exhibits in a very marked manner, however, the projection of the superior part of the occipital bone beyond the occipital spine which characterises the other skulls, and it retains a strong resemblance to them in its other peculiarities.

"The Muskham skull was found associated with bones of the *Bos longifrons*, goat, red-deer, wolf, and dog; so that neither on this ground, nor on any other that I am acquainted with, does there seem to be any good reason for assigning to it a date earlier than the historic, or immediately pre-historic, epoch.

"I have dwelt thus long upon the Muskham skull because of its comparatively perfect condition, and because, so far as the imperfect condition of the fragments from Heathery Burn Cave allows me to judge, they appear to belong to the same race of rather small and lightly-made men, with prominent supraciliary ridges and projecting nasal bones. The few animal remains associated with them are all of recent species, and I see no reason for believing them to be of older date than the river-bed skulls."

One of the Towyn-y-Capel skulls, mentioned above, is represented in figs. 52-55.

An account of the discovery of these skulls by the Hon. W. O. Stanley, entitled "Towyn-y-Capel and the ruined Chapel of St. Bride, on the West Coast of Holyhead Island, with notices of the curious interments there discovered," is published in the third volume of the "Archæological Journal of the Archæological Institute," 1846. The graves are contained in a mound of sand, 30 feet high by 750 in circumference; and are disposed in four or five tiers, one above another, at intervals of three or four feet. Each grave was commonly formed of about twelve flat stones, three on either side, three at the bottom, and three at the top; and no clothing, weapons, or ornaments were discovered in them. According to tradition, a battle took place here in the fifth century, between the Irish and the Welsh. If the interments in question really followed upon this event, it is possible that the skull figured is an Irish skull. The cephalic index of the Towyn-y-Capel skull (5712 M. Mus. Coll. Chir.) is 7.2. The calvarial sutures are all open, and the bones which they unite have become partially separated. There is a curious, deeply constricted, Wormian bone in the outer half of each crus of the lambdoidal suture. The parietal foramina are inconspicuous. The *probole* is well developed, and the *norma occipitalis* (fig. 56) sharply pentagonal.

Of the Irish crania referred to I have here given figures of the most characteristic, the one from the river Blackwater in Armagh, the other the remarkable skull from Borris.

The Blackwater skull (figs. 56–59) is, it will be observed, strikingly similar to the Muskham cranium in its general characters. A second skull from the same locality has the same features, but is still wider, its index amounting to .80. Of the skulls from the bed of the Nore, at Borris, one, with a general similarity to the foregoing, has a strongly developed *probole* and a cephalic index of only .738. The larger skull from the same locality is one of the most remarkable European skulls I have met with. Two views of it are given in figs. 60, 61.

This skull is 8 in. long, and 5.9 in. broad, whence its cephalic index is .737. The height from the front margin of the occipital foramen to the vertex is only 5.45 inches, or 0.68 of the length, so that the skull is greatly depressed. The supraciliary ridges are prominent, the forehead retreating, the *probole* large, and the superior curved line and occipital spine well marked. The supra-auditory ridges are strong, the mastoid processes well developed, and that on the left side somewhat recurved at it apex. The axis of the occipital foramen inclines, if anything, a little backwards. The lower jaw is wanting, as well as the right upper maxilla, and all the alveolar part of the left. But the left jugal arch and orbit and the upper part of the nasal bones, are preserved. The strength of the zygoma is notable, but its projection is more forward than lateral, so that it is hardly seen in the *norma verticalis*. The face must have been very prognathous.

So far as I can judge from the cast, neither the coronal, sagittal, nor lambdoidal sutures are completely closed in this skull. A strong depression or groove follows the course of the sagittal suture.

From what has been stated above, it would appear that the ancient Irish skull was predominantly dolichocephalic, more so even than the ancient Scotch skull. The contrary opinion seems to have generally prevailed, to some extent, I think, in consequence of a mistake on the part of Retzius, who ascribes to the Phœnix Park skull a cephalic index of .82, while it is really, according to Messrs. Davis and Thurnam, only .79. Of the two skulls found in the Knockmaraidhe tumulus, near Dublin, the cephalic index of the one not figured in the "Crania Britannica" is .77, while that of the figured example is only .73. Of these crania, Dr. Davis remarks: "We may well believe that in these skulls we have the most faithful and the most intimate representations of the aborigines of Ierne that can be revealed to the light of modern days. Every evidence educed by the opening of the Knock-maraidhe kistvaen goes to confirm this. No appearance whatever renders it probable that the sepulchral chamber had been disturbed since the day on which the tumulus was raised. Even the secondary interments met with on the outskirts of the mound are unequivocally of the primeval period; and these cistic tombs themselves, constructed according to the customs of incremation, when this practice prevailed, are most likely subsequent, perhaps by a considerable time, to the large kistvaen. This latter, so carefully built and covered by so vast a mound of earth and stones, in every feature speaks of the most remote antiquity; the brief space of its chamber, the contracted position of the bodies thrust into it, and the objects found with them—the flint speculum, the bone pin, and shell necklace—the constant coincidents of pristine rudeness among all uncivilised tribes, all concur in this testimony." ("Crania Britannica," Decade III.)

Sir W. Wilde speaks of long-headed, dark, Irish (Firbolgs) west of the Shannon, and of a more globular-headed, light-haired, stock north-east of that river. But I imagine that by "globular-headed" Sir. W. Wilde means only that the people in question have broader heads than the others —not that there was any really brachycephalic stock in Ireland. At any rate, Sir William claims the Uley Barrow skull as that of "a fellow-countryman," and the cephalic index of this skull is only .71. And, according to Dr. J. B. Davis, the mean cephalic index of fourteen male skulls from the old Abbeys of Mayo, Galway, Avonmore, and Kerry, is .750: that of thirty-two living men in Kerry being .776. ("Crania Britannica," Decade VI.)

As the evidence stands at present, I am fully disposed to

identify the ancient population of Ireland with the "long-barrow" and "river-bed" elements of the population of England, and with the long-headed, or "cumbecephalic" inhabitants of Scotland; and to believe that the "round-barrow," or Belgic, element of the Britannic people never colonised Ireland in sufficient numbers to make its presence ethnically felt.

Reviewing the forms of ancient elongated skulls observed in Britain and Ireland, it appears to me that a middle form, and two, or perhaps three, extremes are distinguishable.

The middle form is the Long-barrow and the River-bed skull, exemplified by the Muskham, Towyn-y-Capel, and Blackwater skulls figured above. One extreme is represented by the low, broad, depressed Borris skull (figs. 60, 61) which, singular as it is, by no means stands alone, but has its analogues in the South German Alt-Lussheim skull of Ecker (*l.c.* Pl. XVI.), and the skull No. III. of Friederichs. Furthermore, the "*Batavus genuinus*" of Blumenbach, the skull from Sennen figured by Mr. Busk ("Natural History Review," 1861, Pl. V., fig. 9), and the cranium, of which a representation is given by Mr. Turner ("The Quarterly Journal of Science," April, 1864, fig. 1), are all similarly elongated depressed crania, with retreating forehead, great supraciliary ridges, and (except the last) large *probole*. Another extreme is the elongated narrow skull from Kinaldie, figured by Drs. Davis and Thurnam. The third, if it may be said to differ essentially from the last, is the "cumbecephalic" skull of Wilson.

Both these last-mentioned types are repeated over and over again in the Hohberg and Grave-row series of the Swiss and South-west German skulls, which, as we have seen reason to believe, are of one and the same class as the Scandinavian skull. This resemblance between some forms of elongated British and Irish skulls and those of Scandinavia, has already been noted by Retzius, who speaks, on more than one occasion, of the likeness between the proper Scandinavian and what he calls the "Celtic" skull; and he mentions (*op. c.* p. 8) that having exchanged, with Sir W. Wilde, a typical Scandinavian for a typical Irish skull, both observers agreed that it would be difficult to find any important difference between the two. Retzius has given good figures of the Scandinavian type, so there is, fortunately, no difficulty in understanding what he means; even had not the characters of that skull been fully defined by Ecker, and its likeness to the Hohberg and Grave-row forms recognised.

Furthermore (as was indeed to be expected from the known relations of the people) there seems to be no character by which the crania of the Anglo-Saxons (which, by the way, are generally more or less prognathous) can be distinguished from those of the Scandinavians. And thus, the elongated ancient crania are traceable from Switzerland to Scandinavia; from Scandinavia to Ireland, where they predominate so as to exclude all others; and to the British Islands and Gaul, where they co-existed with (whether they preceded or not) a broad-headed stock.

The Scandinavians form at present a sort of ethnological island. On the east, they are bounded by Finns and Slavonians; on the south, by the central and southern Germans, who, though similar in complexion, are different in cranial form. In ancient times they were an encroaching race—extending, as Saxons and Frisians, to the right bank of the Rhine; and stretching far south and west as Alemanni, Franks, and Normans; while southward and eastward they overlapped the Slavonians. Manifest traces of them are left in all the regions indicated; but whence they came, and how far they and the original Goths and Germans are of one and the same stock, are problems which seem to be beyond solution at present. On the north, the Scandinavians are sharply defined in stature, complexion, and cranial form against the Lapps; nor have they any neighbours nearer than Greenland on the one hand, or north-eastern Asia on the other, who at all approach them in cranial character. However, in Greenland, the Esquimaux have skulls which are in many respects very similar to those of the European long-heads; except that the jugal arches of the European are hardly ever, if ever, so wide and everted as those of some Esquimaux.

But, if it be true, as I believe it is, that close craniological affinities unite the Hiberno-British long-heads on the one hand with the Scandinavians, is it not equally true that as close affinities connect the dolichocephali of our islands with a southern type? On this point I must again quote Dr. Thurnam: "During the last summer I had the advantage of examining the series of sixty Basque skulls, lately added to the collection of the Anthropological Society of Paris. I was at once struck with their great resemblance to the dolichocephalic skulls from the long barrows of this country, and this impression was much confirmed by the perusal of the two memoirs on these skulls by M. P. Broca, so rich in details necessary for the comparison before us." (*l.c.* p. 41,42).

And Dr. Thurnam is evidently inclined to carry on this line of affinity to the ancient Iberians and Phœnicians. I am by no means disposed to stop even here. The same form of skull appears in the "type grossier" of the ancient Egyptian: I suspect it will be found in the inhabitants of Southern Hindustan: and it is finally traceable to Australia, the natives of which country, as I have already pointed out, in the largely developed *probole*, the wall-sidedness, pentagonal *norma occipitalis*, prognathism, and strong brow ridges, and even in the remarkable vertical depression exhibited by some extreme forms of their skulls, come nearest to the ancient long skulls of Europe. In order to render the amount of this resemblance to the river-bed forms obvious, I have figured (figs. 62–65) an Australian cranium in the Museum of the Royal College of Surgeons (No. 5334 C), which happens to have the jaw broken away in the same fashion as most of the river-bed skulls. If the reader will make a tracing of the different views of this skull on transparent paper, and will apply the outlines thus obtained, over the corresponding views of the Muskham, Towyn-y-Capel, Blackwater, No. 8 and No. 2 Keiss skulls, he will, I think, be surprised at the extensive coincidences of form. The *norma occipitalis* is more sharply pentagonal in the Australian skull, owing to the flattening of the parietal bones; and the frontal region is a little higher and narrower in proportion; but the differences between different Australian skulls, in these respects, are far greater than those between the Australian and the European. It is worth noting that, in the skull figured, the sagittal, lambdoidal, and occipito-mastoid sutures are open throughout; while the left end of the coronal is closed for more than an inch, and the right end is nearly closed.

Some of the skulls from Nordendorf, and the Swedish skulls, figured by Ecker, are, in contour and proportions characteristically Australioid. The Neanderthal skull, as I have elsewhere shown, is more nearly approached by existing Australian skulls, than by any other; and though the Australian cranium hardly attains the breadth of the Ledbury and Borreby skulls, it is singular how closely some Australian skulls approach them in longitudinal contour.

So far as cranial characters go then, it appears to me that all the people whom I have enumerated are affined, but the ethnological value to be attached to the osteological resemblances will depend upon a number of considerations.

It does not seem to be more difficult to admit that two sections of mankind may be very similar cranially, and yet very different in other respects, than it is to believe—as the facts compel us to do—that the lion and the tiger, the fox and the jackal, the ass and the zebra, are far more strikingly differentiated by their pelage than by their skulls. In fact, looking at ethnological classification as a whole, the conclusion of Bory de St. Vincent, and others, that it is the hair and skin which give us characters of primary importance, while osteological peculiarities are secondary, seems to be inevitable.

Admitting Bory de St. Vincent's two primary divisions of the genus *Homo*, the *Leiotrichi*, or smooth-haired, and the *Ulotrichi*, or crisp-haired,—the *Leiotrichi* may be best subdivided, according to their complexion, into *Xanthochroi*,* *Melanochroi*, *Xanthomelanoi*, and *Melanoi*. In several, if not the whole, of these secondary divisions, tertiary divisions based upon the form of the skull may be established, thus:

LEIOTRICHI.

XANTHOCHROI	*Brachycephali,*	*Ex.*	Belgæ; Modern S. Germans and Swiss; Fins, Slavonians.
	Dolichocephali.	*Ex.*	Scandinavians.
MELANOCHROI	*Brachycephali,*	*Ex.*	?
	Dolichocephali,	*Ex.*	Silures, Iberians, Ancient Egyptians. Dark Aryans generally(?)
MELANOI	*Dolichocephali,*	*Ex.*	Drawidians. Australians.
	Brachycephali,	*Ex.*	?
XANTHOMELANOI	*Dolichocephali,*	*Ex.*	Esquimaux, Tunguses (?) Americans, Polynesians.
	Brachycephali,	*Ex.*	Mongolians.

It will be observed, in this table, that the existence of brachycephali in either the *Melanochroi*, or *Melanoi*, is marked as doubtful; by which I mean to indicate, not that people of this coloured hair and complexion may not occasionally have a cephalic index of 0.8; nor that people with broad heads, like

* See "On the Methods and Results of Ethnology," *Fortnightly Review*, No. III.

the Thibetans, may not occasionally have dark skins; but that brachycephaly, and still more brachistocephaly, is a rare phenomenon among these two groups. Among the *Xanthomelanoi* of America (excluding the Esquimaux) and of Polynesia, both dolichocephaly and brachycephaly are found, though the latter predominates.

It further appears that though the Esquimaux, the Scandinavians, the Iberians, and the Australians are all dolichocephalic, and present other points of similarity in cranial structure, they respectively belong to different divisions of the *Leiotrichi*, and must be regarded as representatives of different sections of mankind, whatever the taxonomic value of those sections may be.

For anything we know, or have other than philological reasons for believing to the contrary, fair brachycephali ("Belgæ," Fins, etc.); fair dolichocephali (Scandinavians); dark but pale-complexioned dolichocephali (Iberians, etc.); and dark and yellow skinned brachycephali (Lapps), may have inhabited some part or other of the area they now respectively occupy in Europe, for long ages before the dawn of history.

Hence, it is worth while to reflect, that the current notions respecting the migrations of races from east to west *may* be myths developed out of the facts of philology; and that successive waves of language may have spread over Europe by washing over, instead of being carried by, its populations.

That this is what has happened and is happening in our own islands appears to me sufficiently probable. Our population contains three distinct ethnological elements: I. *Xanthochroi brachycephali*; II. *Xanthochroi dolichocephali*; and III. *Melanochroi*. In Cæsar's time, and for an indefinitely long preceding period, Gaul contained the first and third of these elements, and the shores of the Baltic presented the second. In other words, the ethnological elements of the Hiberno-British Islands are identical with those of the nearest adjacent parts of the continent of Europe, at the earliest period when a good observer noted the characters of their population.

Dr. Thurnam has adduced many good reasons for believing that the "Belgic" element intruded upon a preexisting dolichocephalic "Iberian" population; but I think it probable that this element hardly reached Ireland at all, and extended but little into Scotland. However, if this were the case, and no other elements entered into the population, the tall, fair, red-haired, and blue-eyed dolichocephali, who are, and appear always to have been, so numerous among the Irish and Scotch, could not be accounted for.

But their existence becomes intelligible, at once, if we suppose that long before the well-known Norse and Danish invasions, a stream of Scandinavians had set in to Scotland and Ireland, and formed a large part of our primitive population. And there can be no difficulty in admitting this hypothesis when we recollect that the Orkneys and the Hebrides have been, in comparatively late historical times, Norwegian possessions.

Admitting that in the prehistoric epoch, central Europe was peopled by short-headed *Xanthochroi;* northern (Baltic) Europe by long-headed *Xanthochroi;* and Western Europe by dolichocephalic *Melanochroi,* the present and past states of the population of the same area become intelligible enough.

In ancient times when, to use Dr. Dasent's words, "Scandinavia was the great slave market of Europe," the introduction of fair *brachycephali* into the Baltic area may as readily be understood (without having recourse to any special "Finnic" hypothesis) as the elimination of this element, and the return of the Scandinavians to the long-headed type, in modern times, when the brachycephalic infusion ceased.

In another fashion, the fair and broad-headed "Belgæ" intruded into the British area; but, meeting with a large dolichocephalic population, which at subsequent times was vastly reinforced by Anglo-Saxon, Norse and Danish invasions, this type has been almost washed out of the British population, which is, in the main, composed of fair dolichocephali and dark dolichocephali.

The reverse process has obtained in central Europe. When the great Teutonic stocks swarmed into the Roman Empire, as the Gauls, with less success, had attacked the Republic, they spread the type of the dolichocephalic *Xanthochroi* far beyond its primitive bounds. But, however they might seem to be conquerors, the Franks and Alemanni, who settled in central Europe, were ethnologically defeated. On their right flank were more numerous "Belgæ" and people of like stock; on the left flank innumerable Slavonians. Under these circumstances, while complexions might remain unchanged, dolichocephaly had no chance against brachycephaly, and accordingly the latter has eliminated the former.

But language has, in no respect, followed these physical changes. The fair *dolichocephali* and fair *brachycephali* of Germany, Scandinavia, and England speak Teutonic dialects; while those of France have a substantially Latin speech ; and the majority of those of Scotland and, within historic times, all those of Ireland, spoke Celtic tongues. As to the *Melanochroi*, some speak Celtic, some Latin, some Teutonic dialects; while others, like the Basques (so far as they come under this category), have a language of their own.

To return from this long digression upon the general characters of the population of Europe to the particular case with the consideration of which I commenced these notes.

None of the skulls from Keiss is a typical example of the "Belgic," or brachycephalic constituent of the British population; No. 7 approaches that type, however, and I suspect exhibits the result of admixture between it and the *dolichocephali*.

Of the three other forms of skull discriminated, I am disposed to doubt whether No. 5 is other than a female modification of the River-bed type, represented by Nos. 8 and 2; and thus the really distinct types would be reduced to the River-bed form and that of No. 1, which, although a female skull, has far other peculiarities than its sexual ones.

The questions arise—are the River-bed skulls and No. 1 simply extreme forms of the same type, or are they substantially different? In the former case, are they Scandinavian or Iberian? in the latter, which is Scandinavian and which Iberian?

Without very much larger data, I should not venture to give any positive answer to either of these questions; but I confess I am greatly disposed towards the hypothesis that, if the two are distinct, the River-bed skull is of Iberian, the other of Scandinavian descent.

B.—The Bones of the Body and Limbs.

Except the pelves (and the other bones in the case of No. 1), these bones are too imperfectly preserved, or too ordinary in character, to admit of, or need, detailed description.

In order to render the significance of the peculiarities of the pelves clear, it will be necessary to put before the reader a brief digest of the present state of knowledge on this subject.

Vrolik, in his "Considerations sur la diversité des Bassins de différentes Races humaines," published in 1826, suggested rather than asserted, the existence of racial differences among the pelves of mankind, running parallel with the racial difference of their skulls discovered by Blumenbach. Weber, ("Die Lehre von den Ur- und Racen-Formen der Schädel und Becken des Menschen,") investigating the same question more thoroughly, distinguished four typical forms of pelvis—1. the *oval;* 2. the *round;* 3. the *quadrate;* and 4. the *wedge-shaped.*

1. In the *oval* type the transverse diameter of the brim exceeds the conjugate, or antero-posterior, diameter. In spaciousness and height this pelvis occupies a middle position between the round and the wedge-shaped. The latter is as a rule narrow and high, the round, on the contrary, is wide and lower. Weber distinguishes, within the limits of this type, the female, *round-oval,* and the male, *oval,* forms without giving any very clear definition of either. As examples he cites the oval pelvis of an European male, with its diameters 4 in. 3 lines : 3 in. 9 lines;* the oval pelvis of a Botocudo, 4 in. 7 lines : 4 in. ; and the transversely oval pelvis of an European female (as an example of the farthest point the oval type can reach without passing into the round) 5 in. : 3 in. 10 lines.

2. In the *round* type the transverse and the conjugate diameters are nearly equal. The examples given are the pelvis of a female European, 4 in. 5 lines : 4 in. 2 lines; and the pelvis of a negress of 37 years of age, 4 in. 7 lines : 4 in. 3 lines.

3. The *quadrate* pelvis is that which is compressed anteriorly, laterally, and posteriorly, but especially in the symphysial region, so that the brim is almost quadrangular.

* For brevity's sake I shall write the two diameters in this way, always putting the transverse first.

The transverse is greater than the conjugate diameter. The examples are, the pelvis of a European woman, 4 in. 11 lines : 3 in. 10 lines ; and Vrolik's two Javanese and one Mestizo pelves (Jav. 4 in. 2 lines : 3 in. 8 lines ; Jav. 4 in. 3 lines : 4 in.; Mest. 5 in. 6 lines : 4 in. 3 lines).

4. The *wedge-shaped* pelvis. This is compressed laterally, so as to be narrower from side to side than from before backwards ; the pubes unite at an acute angle, and the horizontal branches of those bones, therefore, take a more straight direction backwards than is the case in the oval pelvis ; the *lineæ arcuatæ* of the sacrum and of the ilia are less excavated. The conjugate is consequently greater than the transverse diameter, and the brim is not oval, but wedge-shaped. The ilia are high and converge considerably below; their distance is consequently less than in any of the preceding forms. When the characters of this pelvis are less distinct and rounded off, it approximates to the oval type. As exemplifications of this type are cited :—The wedge-shaped pelvis of a European woman, exhibiting the most extreme form of this pelvis which had fallen within Weber's observation. The diameters are 4 in. 6 lines : 4 in. 9 lines. The pelvis of a Botocudo woman, 4 in. 3 lines : 4 in. 6 lines. The pelvis of a Caffre, 3 in. 9 lines : 4 in. Weber adds the outlines of the brim of the pelvis of a negress in Von Sœmmering's collection (3 in. 9 lines : 3 in. 11 lines), and that of the pelvis of one of Vrolik's negroes.

The general conclusion which Weber draws is, that any form of pelvis may occur in any race; but that "as in Europeans the oval type is that which occurs most frequently, so the round form is the primitive type of the American race, the quadrate that of the Mongolian race, and the cuneiform that of the Æthiopian race ; and that, in each of these races, the typical form is that which presents itself most frequently, though it does not exclusively occur. In

Europeans, according to my observations, after the oval form the round, after that the square, and most rarely the cuneiform type occurs. How it may be with other races I cannot say."

Since Weber, the only author who has devoted a treatise to this subject is Dr. Joulin, who, in his "Memoire sur le Bassin considéré dans les Races Humaines," published in the "Archives Générales de Medicine," for 1864, endeavours to prove that the most important anatomical peculiarities which have been affirmed to characterise Negro and Mongolian pelves do not exist; that the slight differences observable in the pelves of the three human races are not characteristic, appearing only when the comparison extends over a number of examples; that the Mongolian and Negro races have indistinguishable pelves; and that, if the form of the cranium leads to the division of man into three principal races, that of the pelvis affords but two groups—the Aryan, and the Mongolic-negro.

However, an objection of some importance must be taken, *in limine*, to these conclusions. Among the "Mongolic" pelves of Dr. Joulin there is not one which belongs to a typical Mongol. Three of the nine are Bushwomen, who are as different from the Mongols as can well be imagined, two are South American, and four are Javanese. There is not a single proper, or continental, Asiatic Mongol on the list. So far as they profess to show the character of the typical Mongolian pelvis, therefore, Dr. Joulin's observations tell us nothing. As to the seventeen so-called Negro pelves, eleven appear to be those of truly African Negresses; but the other six belong not to Negroes, but to Negritoes, one being Papuan, the others New Caledonian.

After criticising Vrolik's statements respecting the characters of the Negro pelvis (and not without justice, though I cannot find in Vrolik's Memoir all of the opinions which Dr. Joulin ascribes to him), Dr. Joulin states—

"I may then assert, in an absolute manner, that, in all the races of mankind, the transverse diameter of the brim of the female pelvis predominates over the conjugate diameter. I know of not a single observation to the contrary; on the other hand, not only does this law apply to the female sex in general, but it is equally applicable to both sexes, and the predominance of the transverse diameter is alike observed in the male. In about sixty subjects which I have examined in reference to this point, I have only met with a single exception, and this was not in a Negro, but in a Caucasian of the Berber division; it is a Kabyle whose pelvis has an altogether peculiar form, explicable only by some anomaly of development. In Negro pelves, I have observed a peculiarity which is very important, for it is almost characteristic—it is the little difference which exists between the oblique and transverse diameters. In the Aryan this difference is fifteen millemetres, in the Negro two, in the Mongol six. This point has not been noted and has escaped Vrolik; its effect is to render the brim a little more square than it is in the white race."

"There is an important point on which Vrolik has not laid sufficient stress: it is that, in capacity, the Negro and Mongolian pelves are inferior to the white in all diameters, except in the antero-posterior diameter of the cavity, and the coccy-pubic of the inferior outlet, which are almost equal in the three races."

I have measured all the pelves of savage races of mankind which have come in my way, and I have collected all the admeasurements by other observers which I have been able to discover. The results as to the relations of the transverse and conjugate diameters of the brim of the pelvis are shown in the following tables, in which I have arranged, in the first two columns, absolute measurements, as given by other observers or taken by myself; and in the last column the *pelvic index*, or ratio of the conjugate diameter to the transverse diameter, taken as unity :—

PELVES OF AFRICAN NEGROES.

12 Females.			6 Males.		
	mm. mm.	index		in. in.	index
Joulin.........No. 2...138 : 134		.97	(Vrolik) No. 1... 4⅓ : 4⅓		103
„ .... 3...128 : 107		.83		in. l. in. l.	
„ .... 4...125 : 100		.80	„ 2...3.10 : 4.0		104
„ .... 5...114 : 110		.96	„ 3...3.10 : 4.0		104
Joulin (Vrolik) 6...119 : 97		.81	Von Sœmmering ...3.11½ : 3.7½		.91
„ „ 7...119 : 102		.85	Male Negro (College in. in.		
Joulin......... 8...126 : 98		.77	of Surgeons Mus.)4.15 : 4.1		.98
Joulin (Vrolik) 9...119 : 97		.81	Male Negro (Wood,		
Joulin......... 10...112 : 104		.92	*l.c.*) .... 3.9 : 4.1		105
„ .... 11...112 : 90		.80			
„ .... 12...103 : 85		.82		mean,	100
	in. in.				
Dr. Hull (Wood*) 4⅛ : 4¾		1.06			
	mean,	.87			

PELVES OF NEGRITOES.

6 Females.			1 Male.		
	mm. mm.	index		in.	in. index
Joulin, New Guinea...135 : 115		.85	Isle of Pines (Mus.		
„ New Caledonia 125 : 125		100	Royal College of		
„ „ 130 : 115		.88	Surgeons) .... 4.55 : 4.45		.97
„ „ 123 : 111		.82			
„ „ 125 : 101		.80			
„ „ 108 : 100		.92			
	mean,	.87			

PELVES OF BUSHMEN.

5 Females.			2 Males.		
	in.	in. index		in.	in. index
Royal Coll. of Sur-			Royal College of Sur-		
geons......No. 1...3.75 : 3.85		102	geons .... 3.6 : 3.3		.91
„ 2...4.35 : 3.75		.86	Dr. Grey's specimen 3.95 : 3.85		.97
Joulin, Hottentot					
Venus... 122 : 89		.73		mean,	94
„ Museum ... 125 : 98		.78			
„ (Vrolik) ... 125 : 103		.82			
	mean,	.84			

* " Cyclopædia of Anatomy."—Article " Pelvis."

PELVES OF AUSTRALIANS.

1 Female.			5 Males.		
	in.	in. index		in.	in. index
Royal College of Surgeons..............5.15 : 4.5		.87	Royal College of Surgeons ......No. 1...4.25 : 4.25		100
			,, 2...4.2 : 4.3		102
			,, 3...4.25 : 4.4		103
			,, 4...4.3 : 4.15		.96
			Middlesex Hospital 3.75 : 3.9		104

mean, 101

On comparing the indices of these twenty-four female and fourteen male pelves, it will be observed that not a single male falls below .90; while in eight, or more than half, the index is at or above 100; or, in other words, in these, the conjugate equals or exceeds the transverse diameter. On the other hand, in the series of female pelves, there are only three (or about 12 per cent.) with an index at or above 100; seventeen (or about 70 per cent.) have it below .90; and only four (or about 16 per cent.) at or above .90 and below 106. Taking an index of .90 as the middle term in the female series, more than two-thirds are below, and less than one-third above, this mean.

In the carefully-written article "Pelvis," in the "Cyclopædia of Anatomy and Physiology," Mr. Wood brings together the average measurements of the male and female European pelvis, as stated by divers authorities, and adds his own results, derived from the measurements of eighteen female and fourteen male, European pelves.

The average dimensions of the transverse and conjugate diameters in the two sexes in Europeans adopted by Meckel, Watt, and Wood are as follows:

	MALE.			FEMALE.		
	in. lines.	in. lines.	index.	in. lines.	in. lines.	index.
Meckel . .	4 . 6 :	4 . 0	.88	5 . 0 :	4 . 4	.86
Watt . .	4 . 6 :	4 . 0	.88	5 . 6 :	4 . 9	.86
Wood . .	4 . 7 :	4 . 0	.87	5 . 2 :	4 . 5	.85
	4 . 6⅓	4 . 0	.876	5 . 2⅔	4 . 6	.856

It is remarkable how closely the indices of the average numbers given by these different observers agree—though the numbers themselves differ a good deal for the female pelvis. Still more singular is the near approximation of the mean index of the European female pelvis (.856) to that of Negresses (.87), Negrito women (.87), Australians (.87), and Bushwomen (.84). Thus, although Dr. Joulin goes too far when he asserts that the conjugate diameter of the female pelvis never exceeds the transverse, he would appear to be fully borne out in his conclusion that the diameters of the brim of the female pelvis do not, on the average, present very great differences in proportion in the different races of mankind. There is some ground for suspecting, however, that the conjugate diameter more frequently bears a large proportion to the transverse in the savage races, than in Europeans.

On the other hand, there is a vast difference between the savage and the European male pelvis. The brim of the latter is much smaller in all its dimensions than the female, but its proportions are very little different. In the savage, on the other hand, there is the further difference, that the conjugate diameter nearly or quite equals, or may frequently exceed, the transverse.

With respect to the male pelves, as I have already said, I find nothing to distinguish them from well formed and strong European male pelves, except that the conjugate diameter of No. 7 is less than usual, so that its index is only .82, while that of No. 8 is .87. They have not the excessively narrow intersciatic diameter which characterises the Australian male pelvis; and though the more perfect one is very like the pelvis of a male Esquimaux in the Museum of the Royal College of Surgeons, I do not know that there is anything specific about the resemblance.

The pelvis of No. 2, so far as the dimensions of its brim

are concerned, agrees with the female European pelvis which Weber figures (Pl. xxix.,*) as the most extreme example of the "wedge-shaped" type. I have seen but two female pelves of other than European origin which in any way approach it; one of these is the pelvis of the Bushwoman in the Royal College of Surgeons, the other that of a female Esquimaux in the same collection. In its general characters, the Esquimaux pelvis comes nearer that of No. 2 than the Bushwoman's.

The height of No. 2 pelvis is about 7.2 in., that of the Esquimaux 6.75; the extreme distance between the outer edges of the iliac crests is only 9.9 in. in the Esquimaux, while it is still less in No. 2 (9.1 in.) In an European woman of nearly the same stature the same measurement gave 11.5 in., and in an Australian 10.8 in.: even in the male Esquimaux it was 10.2 in. Again, the Esquimaux pelvis has the sciatic notch almost as open as that of No. 2; the distance from the edge of the acetabulum to the nearest point of the fifth sacral vertebra (a measurement which roughly expresses the openness of the notch), being 4 in. in the Esquimaux as against 4.25 in. in No. 2. In this width of the sciatic notch, which, in a less degree, is eminently characteristic of the female pelvis, in general, the pelves of the male and female Esquimaux are as strongly contrasted as those of No. 7 and No. 2.

The pelvis of the female Esquimaux further departs from the ordinary type in the circumstance that, while the transverse diameter of the brim is 4.7 in., the conjugate is 4.6 in., or very nearly equal to the former. Again, the antero-posterior measurement of the cavity of the pelvis is great, amounting to as much as 5.45. in. On the other hand, the sub-pubic arch is tolerably wide, its angle amounting to fully 90°.

* Marked xxviii. by mistake in the original.

In such respects as the pelvis of No. 2 differs from that of Esquimaux it departs further from the ordinary character. The transverse diameter of the brim is slightly narrower (4.6 in.), the conjugate diameter three-tenths of an inch longer (4.9 in.); the index therefore = 104. The antero-posterior measurement of the true pelvis is an inch greater. The sub-pubic angle is acute. In this point, the pelvis of No. 2 differs from the Bushwoman's pelvis as well as from the Esquimaux's; and, in fact, the acuteness of the pubic arch of No. 2 long led me to doubt its being a female pelvis.

While the pelvis No. 2 is, if I may use the expression, some distance on the abnormal side of the Esquimaux, that of No. 1 approaches near to the normal type. The width of the haunches is the same as in the Esquimaux; the sciatic notch is about as open; the antero-posterior diameter of the cavity may have been very similar. On the other hand, the transverse diameter of the brim is greater, so that the brim more nearly approaches the ordinary transversely oval form. It is to be recollected, however, that in this pelvis, as it is now restored and figured, the symphysial interval is certainly too great, and that every diminution of this interval would increase the conjugate and lessen the transverse diameter. In other words, the difference between it and the Esquimaux would certainly have been lessened had the pelvis been entire. I did not feel justified in giving the parts any other position than that into which they fall, when coadapted in their present condition.

It would be very unsafe to assume that the peculiar forms of the single female Esquimaux pelvis, and of the two Keiss pelves, are other than accidental. And yet until they are shown to be accidental, by the examination of a greater number of pelves of both kinds, I think the fact, as it stands, must be carefully borne in mind.

Since this passage was written, Mr. Turner has supplied

me with the measurements of the only other female pelvis obtained from Keiss, given above at p. 99. The pelvic index is .97. In other words, it exhibits the same remarkable peculiarity as the others; and thus of the known three female pelves from Keiss, the pelvic index of two is far above .90, and that of the third is not below .90; while had they been pelves of savage races, only one should have been in this position; and had they been modern European pelves, it may be doubted if, on the ordinary doctrine of chances, one in twenty should have had this conformation..

I have compared the bones of the limbs and spine of No. 1 with the corresponding parts of the skeleton of a well-formed European female, and of the female Australian, in the Museum of the Royal College of Surgeons. As mounted, each of these skeletons stands about 5 ft. 2 in. high.

The calcaneum of the European is broad, and from the lower edge of the cuboidal facet to the extreme end of the calcaneal process measures 2.55. In No. 1 it is narrower, and measures 2.75 in length. In the Australian, the same measurement gives 2.9. On the whole, I should say that the calcaneum of No. 1 is somewhat narrower and longer than the average European heel-bone.

The tibia of the European female measured from the femoral to the astragalar articular surfaces, along its posterior face, is 13.4 in. long; in No. 1, 13.2 in.; in the Australian, 13.9 in. There is nothing remarkable about this bone in No. 1.

The fibula in the European is 13.2 in. long; in No. 1 it has the same length; while in the Australian it is 14 in. long. In the European and the Australian its shaft has the ordinary trihedral form, the posterior surface being tolerably flat and broad. In No. 1, on the other hand, this face is very narrow, and the outer surface of the shaft is broad and deeply excavated, so that the bone has quite a peculiar aspect.

The femur of the European, measured along a straight line drawn from the upper surface of the head to a flat surface on which both condyles rest, is 16.7 in. long (proportional, according to the ordinary rule, to a stature of 60.07 in.); that of No. 1 measures only 15.9 in. (proportional to a stature of 57.8 in.); that of the Australian measures 17.3 in. (proportional to a stature of 62.9 in.). Thus supposing the rule of proportion, as length of femur : length of body :: 275 : 1000, to hold good, the Australian ought to be tallest, the European next, and No. 1 last. As a matter of fact, the European skeleton stands a little higher than the Australian. And it will be observed that the fibula and tibia of No. 1, instead of being shorter than those of the European, are exactly of the same length.

So far as this may show a tendency of the distal division of the extremity to bear an increased proportion to the proximal division, it is a character of degradation. At the same time, it indicates that the stature of No. 1 was probably higher than the calculation would make it.

But this character is not repeated in the upper extremities. The radius of No. 1 is 8.75 in. long from the centre of one articular face to that of the other, and that of the European has the same length. That of the Australian measures 9.35.

The humerus, from the centre of the upper surface of the head to the middle of the distal articular surface, is, in both the European and No. 1, 11.7 in., while, in the Australian, it measures 12.25 in.

While the bones of the upper extremity of No. 1 are very similar to those of the European woman, except that they are stronger, and have better developed ridges and processes, the clavicles are very different (fig. 30). They are 5.5 in. in extreme length, while neither the European nor the Australian clavicles exceed 5.3 in. ; and, furthermore, they are much stronger and more curved bones, more like male than female clavicles. The scapulæ of No. 1 are also decidedly long in proportion to their height.

Putting all the elements of the picture together, No. 1, with her long shins and heels, narrow hips, relatively broad shoulders, retreating forehead and projecting jaws, can hardly have been either a graceful, or a comely, personage.

In the spinal column the bodies of the vertebræ have the same size as those of the European female, but the processes are coarser and stronger, and the lower oblique processes of the last lumbar are unusually far apart. The transverse processes of this vertebra are also somewhat stouter and coarser; but they exhibit no such sacrum-like enlargement as is not unfrequently seen in the Bushmen and Australians.

The Skull No. 7.

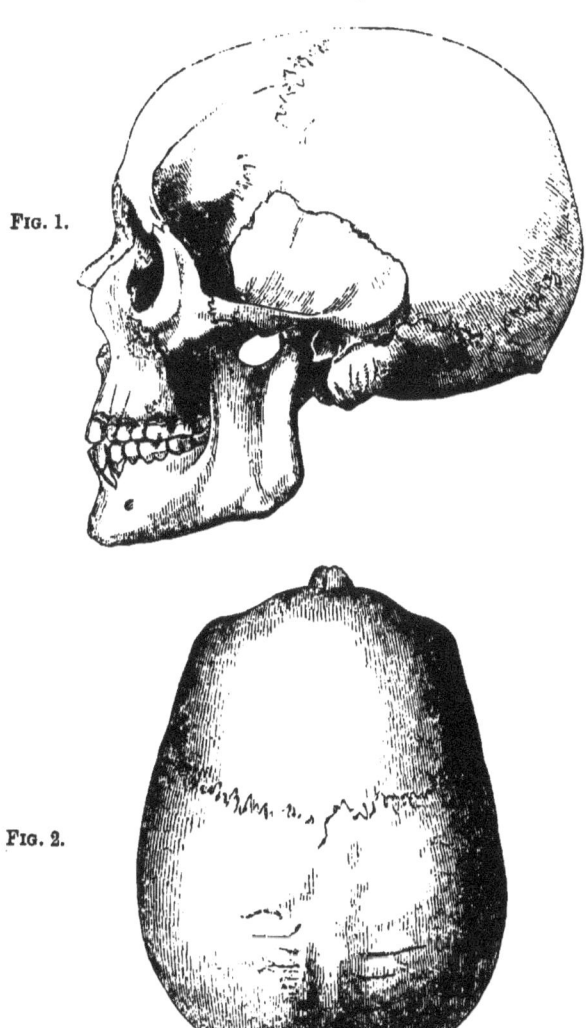

FIG. 1.—*Norma lateralis.*   FIG. 2.—*Norma verticalis.*

⁎ In the lateral, front, and back views of this and all other skulls figured, Mr. Busk's method of placing the skull has been adopted. A plane traversing the auditory meatuses and the junction of the coronal and sagittal sutures is vertical. In the "norma verticalis" the centre of such a plane is traversed by the line of sight. All the drawings are reduced to one-third of the natural size of the skulls.

The Skull No. 7.

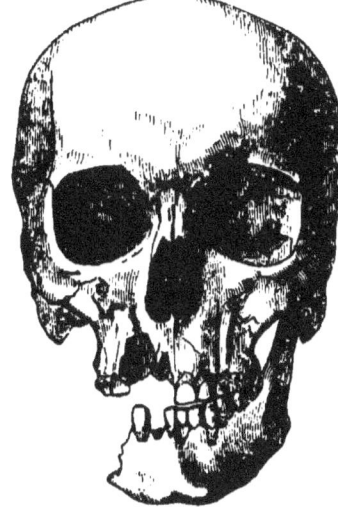

Fig. 3.

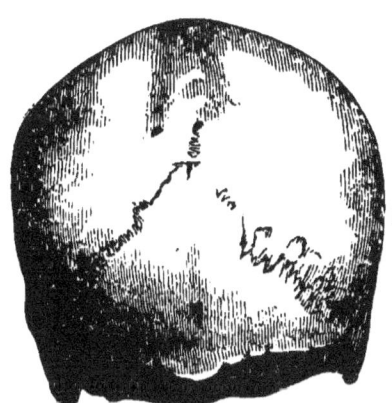

Fig. 4.

Fig. 5.

Fig. 3.—*Norma frontalis.*   Fig. 4.—*Norma occipitalis.*
Fig. 5.—*The palate.*

Pelvis of No. 7.

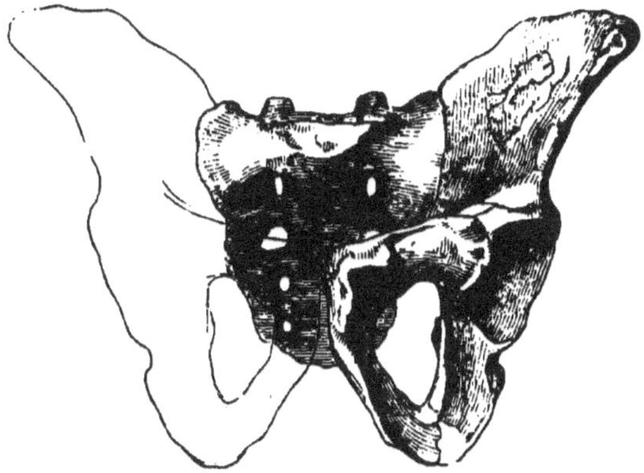

FIG. 6.

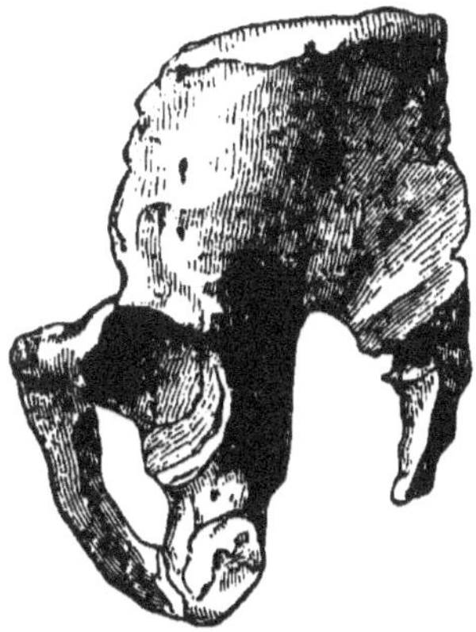

FIG. 7.

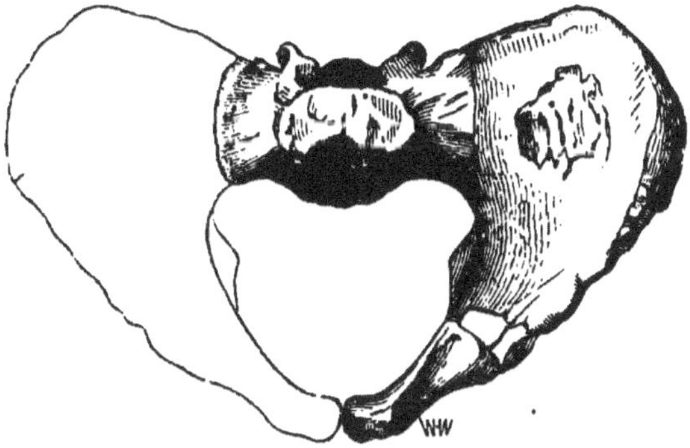

FIG. 8.

FIG. 6.—*Front view.*   FIG. 7.—*Side view.*
FIG. 8.—*View perpendicular to the plane of the brim.*

*⁎** In these and all the other figures of pelves, the front and side views are taken from the pelvis in such a position that the body of the ischium is vertical. The figures are one-fourth of the natural size.

The Skull No. 8.

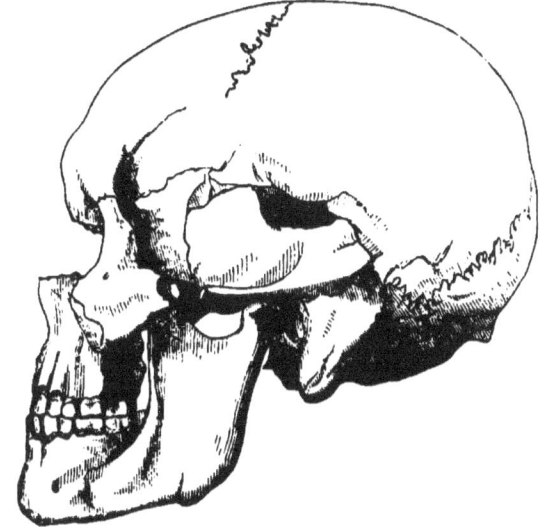

Fig. 9.

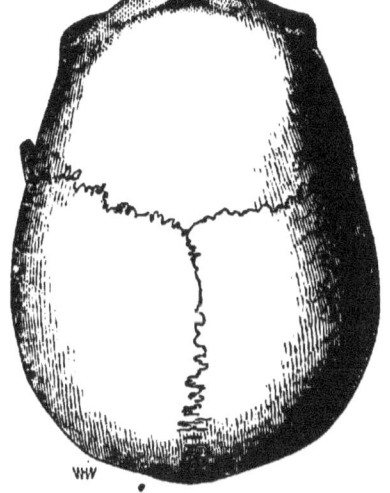

Fig. 10.

Fig. 9.—*Norma lateralis.* Fig. 10.—*Norma verticalis*

The Skull No. 8.

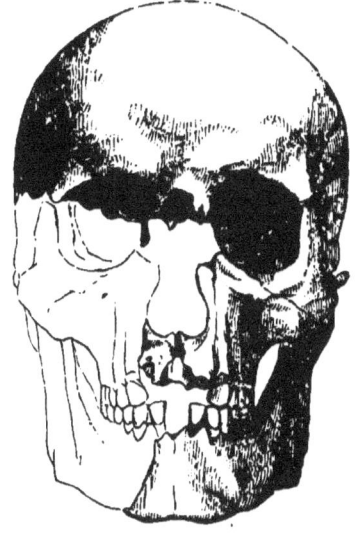

Fig. 11.

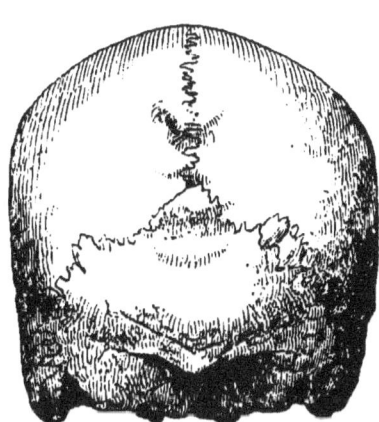

Fig. 12.

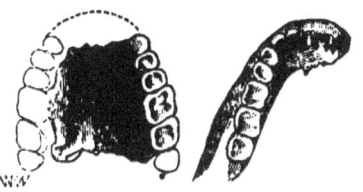

Fig. 13.

Fig. 11.—*Norma frontalis.*   Fig. 12.—*Norma occipitalis.*
Fig. 13.—*Palate and part of the lower jaw.*

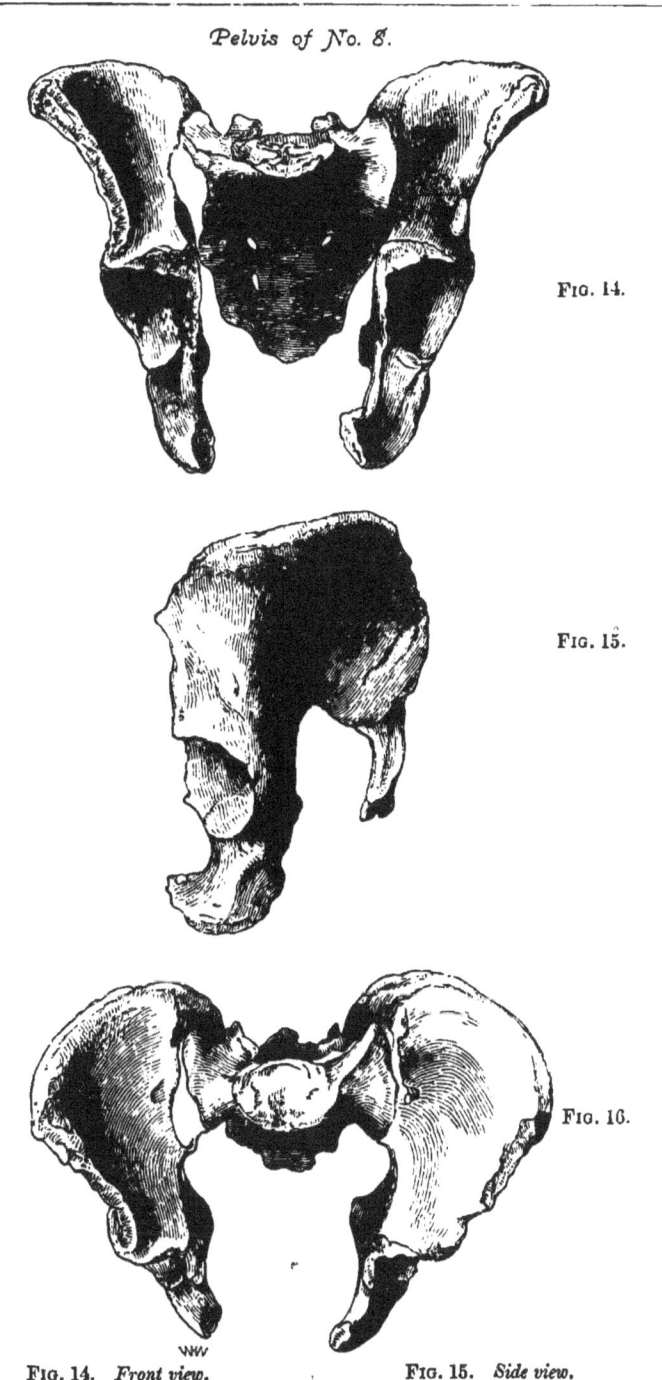

FIG. 14. *Front view.*   FIG. 15. *Side view.*
FIG. 16. *View perpendicular to the plane of the brim.*

The Skull No. 2.

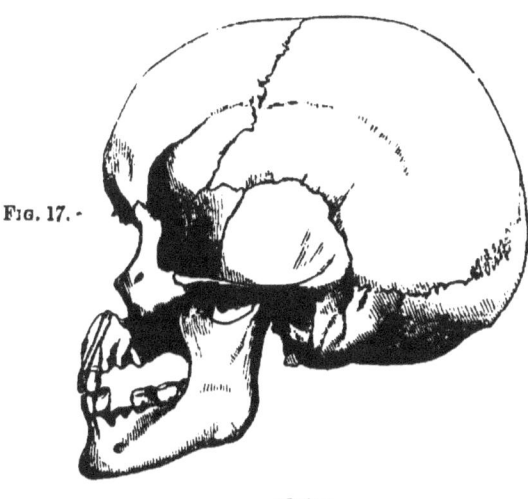

Fig. 17.

Fig. 18.

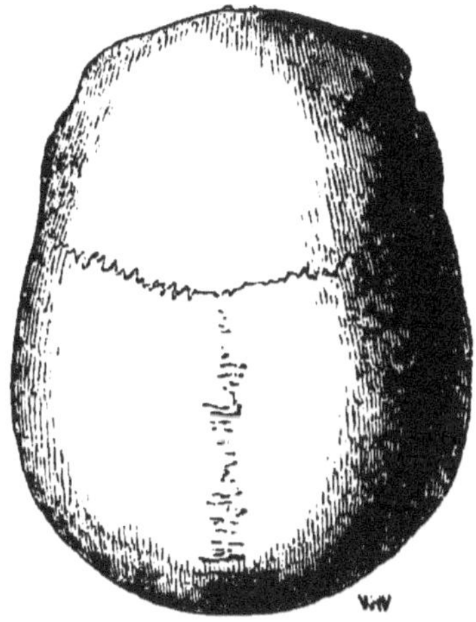

Fig. 17.—*Norma lateralis.*   Fig. 18.—*Norma verticalis.*

The Skull No. 2.

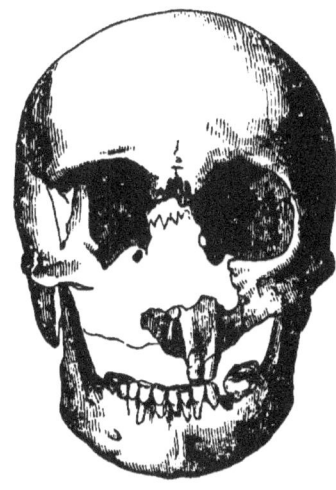

FIG. 19.

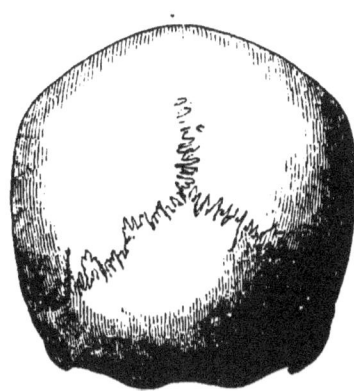

FIG. 20.

FIG. 21.

FIG. 19.—*Norma frontalis.*   FIG. 20.—*Norma occipitalis.*
FIG. 21.—*Palate and horizontal rami of the lower jaw.*

Pelvis of No. 2.

Fig. 22.

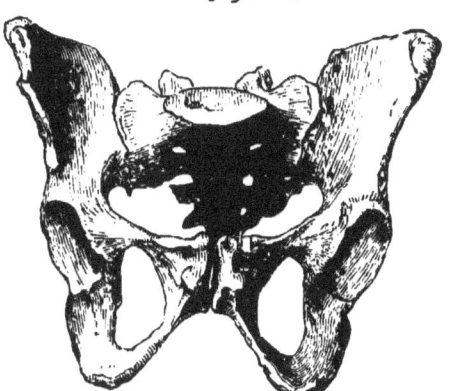

Fig. 23.

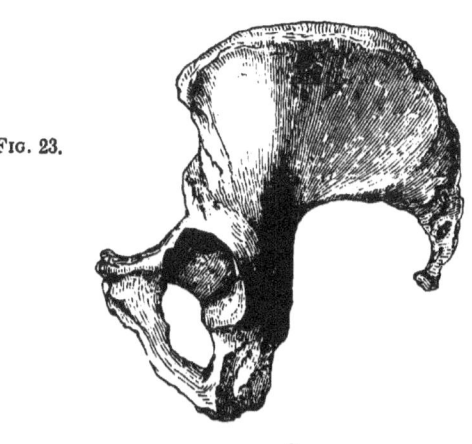

Fig. 24.

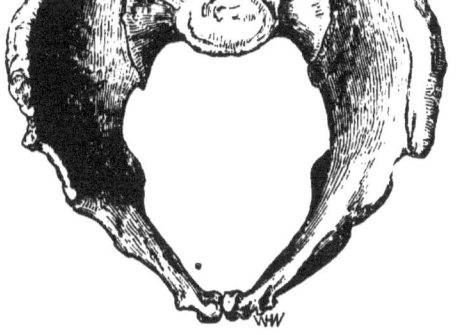

FIGS. 22, 23, 24.—*Three views corresponding with those given in* FIGS. 6, 7, 8.

The Skull No. 1.

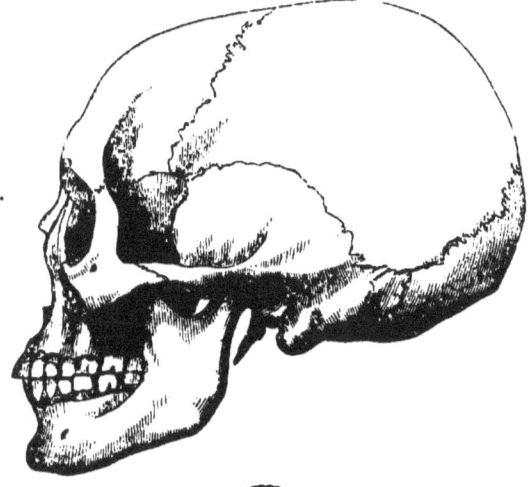

FIG. 25.

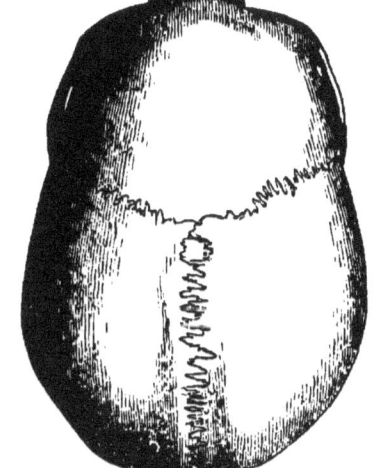

FIG. 26.

FIG. 25.—*Norma lateralis.*   FIG. 26.—*Norma verticalis.*

The Skull No. 1.

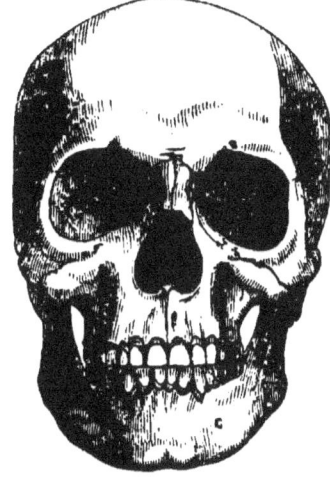

FIG. 27.

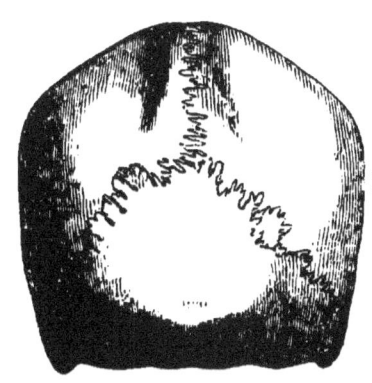

FIG. 28.

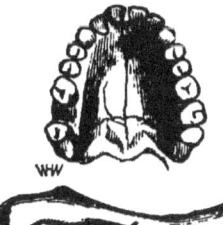

FIG. 29.

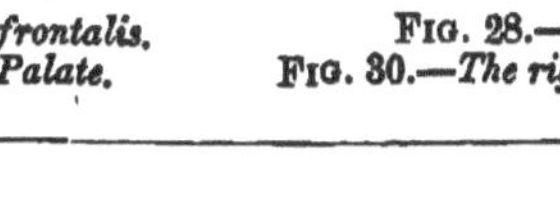

FIG. 30.

FIG. 27.—*Norma frontalis.* FIG. 28.—*Norma occipitalis.*
FIG. 29.—*Palate.* FIG. 30.—*The right clavicle.*

Pelvis of No. 1.

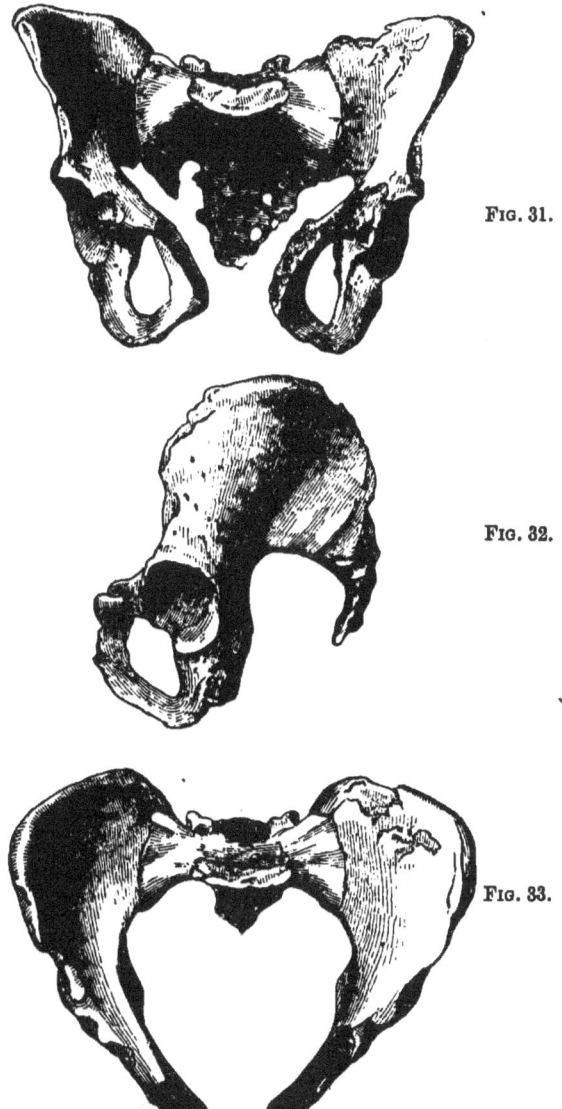

FIG. 31.

FIG. 32.

FIG. 33.

FIGS. 31, 32, 33.—*Three views corresponding with those given in* FIGS. 6, 7, 8.

The Skull No. 3.

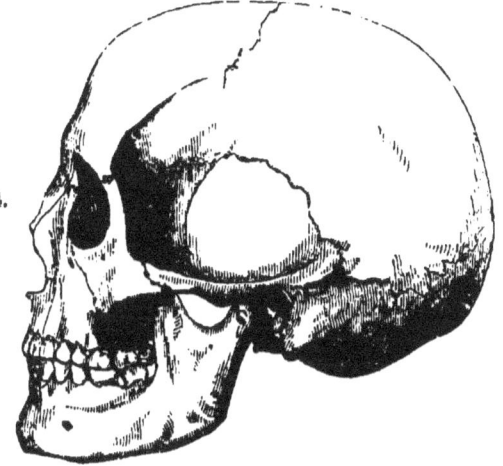

Fig. 34.

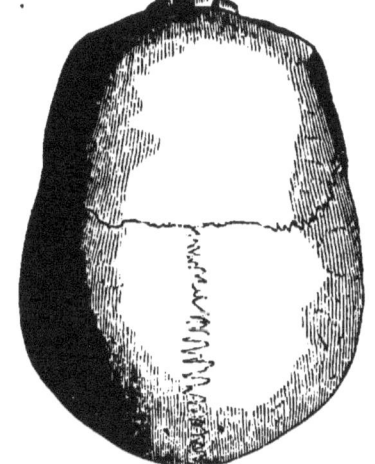

Fig. 35.

Fig. 34.—*Norma lateralis.*   Fig. 35.—*Norma verticalis.*

The Skull No. 3.

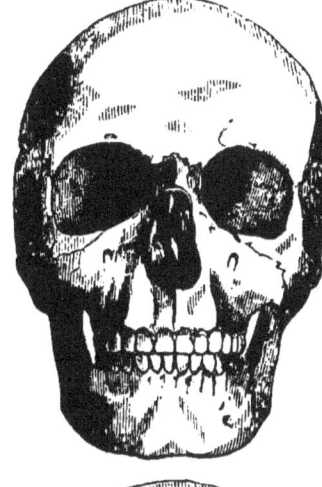

Fig. 36.

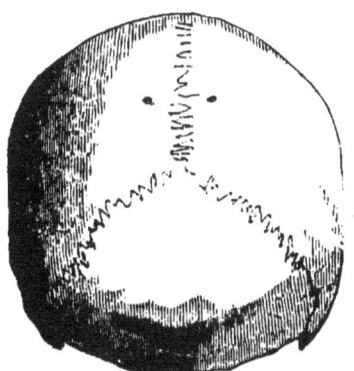

Fig. 37.

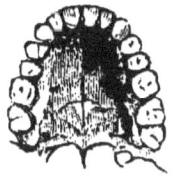

Fig. 38.

Fig. 36.—*Norma frontalis.*   Fig. 37.—*Norma occipitalis.*
Fig. 38.—*The palate.*

The Skull No. 5.

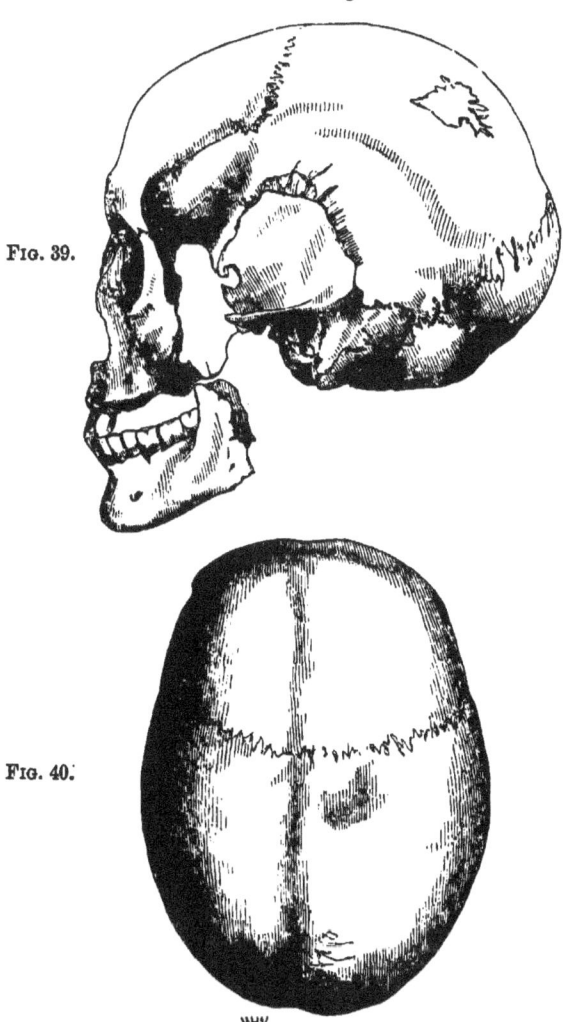

FIG. 39.

FIG. 40.

FIG. 39.—*Norma lateralis.*   FIG. 40.—*Norma verticalis.*

The right half of this skull happens to be more perfect than the left.—In the *norma lateralis*, therefore, the right half of the skull has been drawn and not reversed, so that it comes out as the left half, and can be compared with the corresponding aspects of the other skulls. The other views of this skull have been taken in the same way.

The Skull No. 5.

Fig. 41.

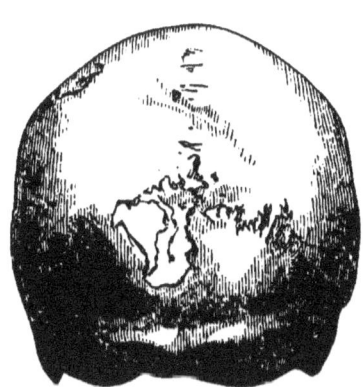

Fig. 42.

Fig. 43.

Fig. 41.—*Norma frontalis.*   Fig. 42.—*Norma occipitalis.*
Fig. 43.—*The palate.*

The Ledbury Skull.

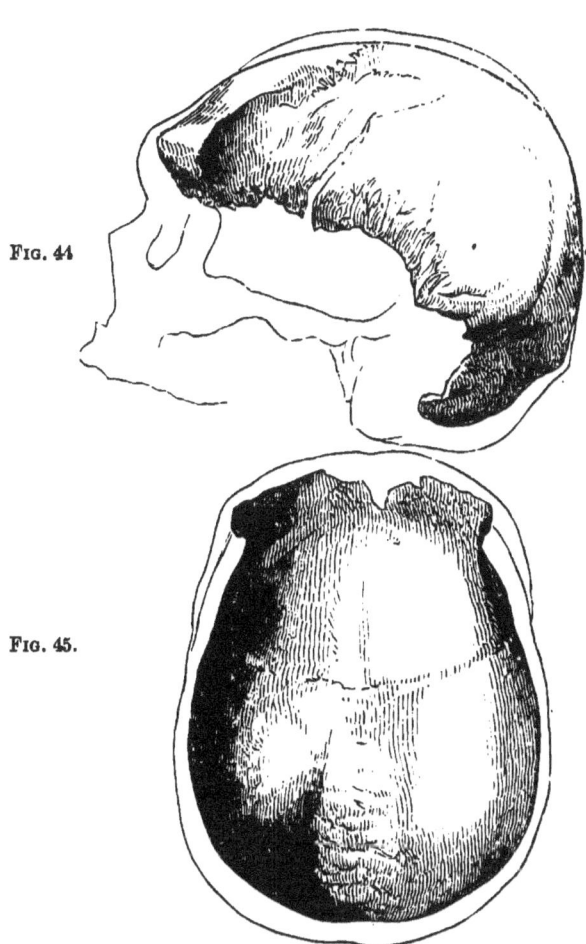

Fig. 44

Fig. 45.

Fig. 44.—*Norma lateralis.*   Fig. 45.—*Norma verticalis.*

The Ledbury Skull.

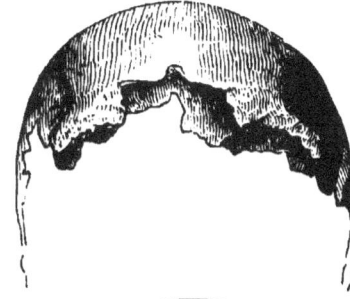

Fig. 46.

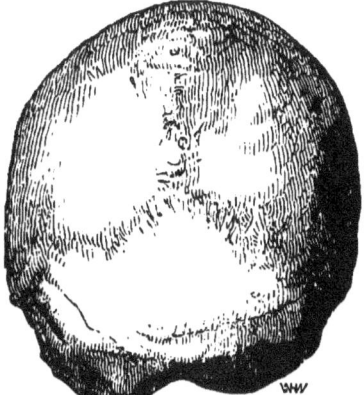

Fig. 47.

Fig. 46.—*Norma frontalis.*   Fig. 47.—*Norma occipitalis.*

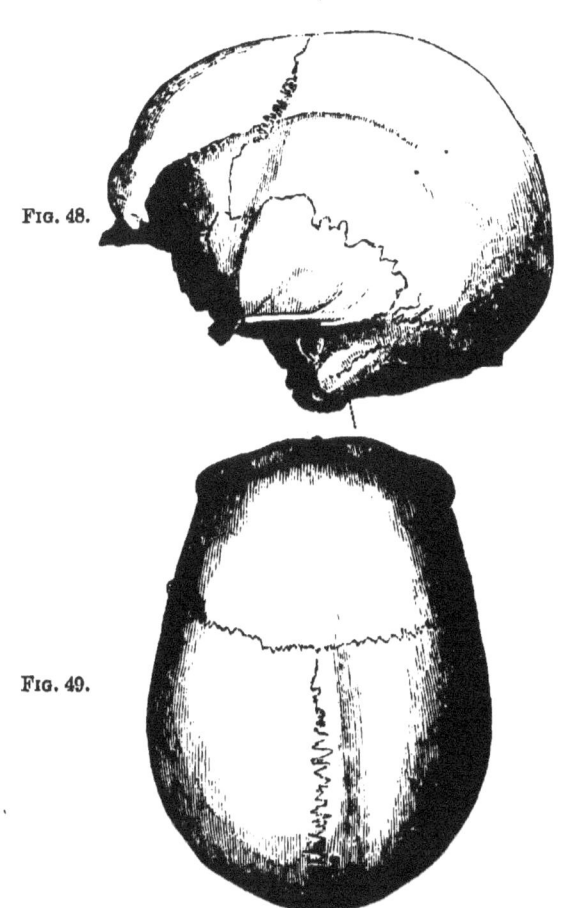

Fig. 48.—*Norma lateralis.*   Fig. 49.—*Norma verticalis.*

The Muskham Skull.

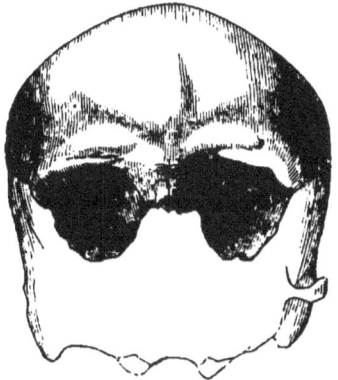

Fig. 50.

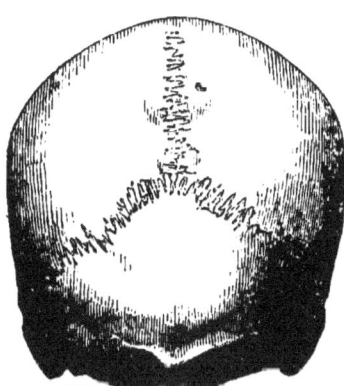

Fig. 51.

Fig. 50.—*Norma frontalis.*   Fig. 51.—*Norma occipitalis.*

The Twyn-y-Capel Skull.

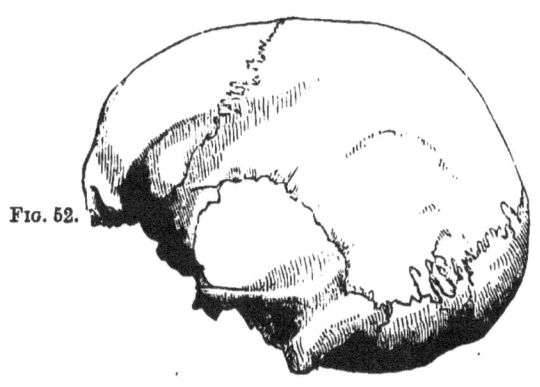

FIG. 52.

FIG. 53.

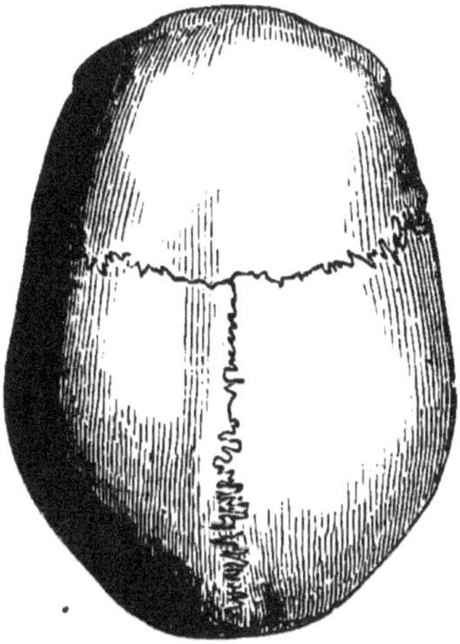

FIG. 52.—*Norma lateralis.*   FIG. 53.—*Norma verticalis.*

The Towyn-y-Capel Skull.

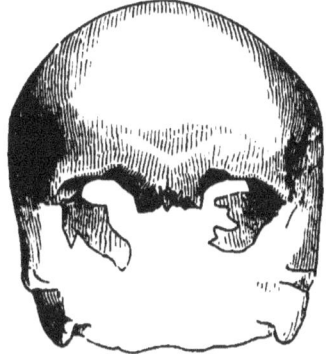

Fig. 54.

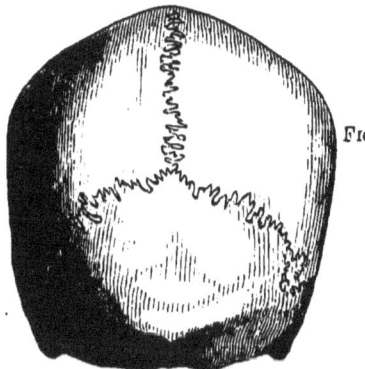

Fig. 55.

Fig. 54.—*Norma frontalis.*   Fig. 55.—*Norma occipitalis.*

The Blackwater River-bed Skull.

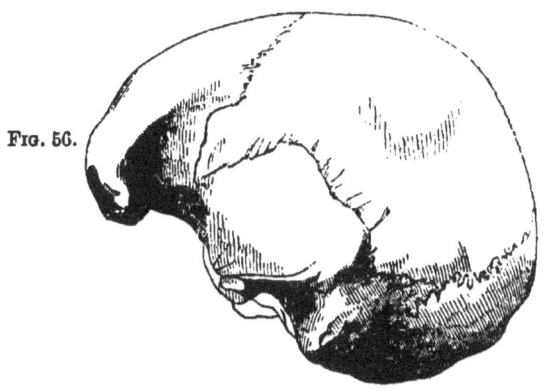

FIG. 56.

FIG. 57.

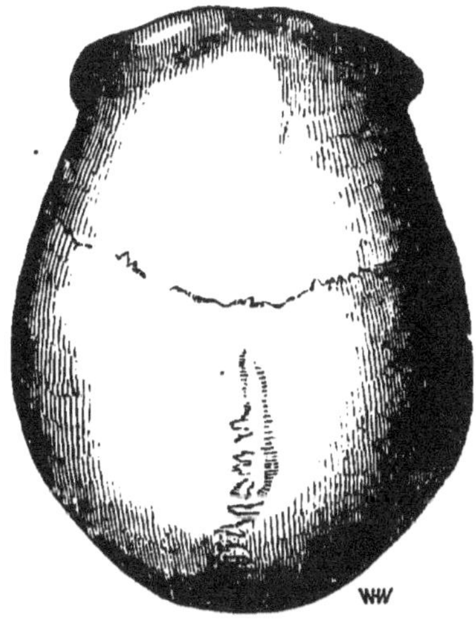

FIG. 56.—*Norma lateralis.*   FIG. 57.—*Norma verticalis.*

The Blackwater River-bed Skull.

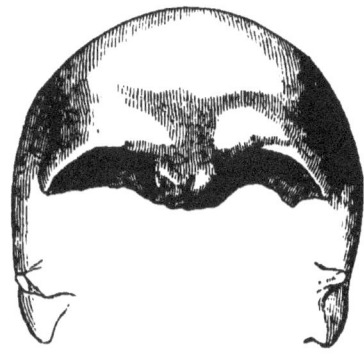

Fig. 58.

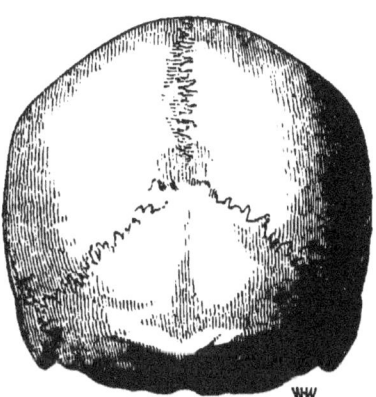

Fig. 59.

Fig. 58.—*Norma frontalis.*   Fig. 59.—*Norma occipitalis.*

The Borris Skull.

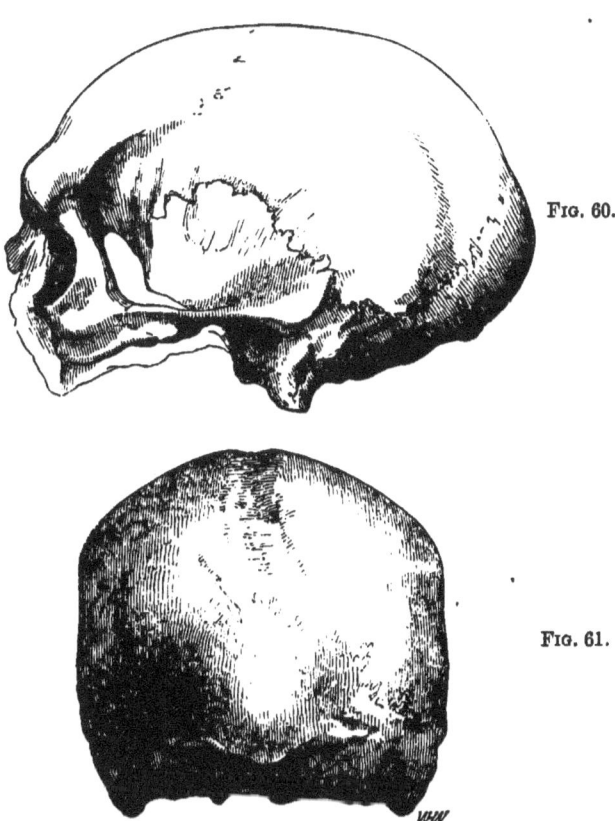

Fig. 60.

Fig. 61.

Fig. 60.—*Norma lateralis.*   Fig. 61.—*Norma occipitalis.*

The Australian Skull.

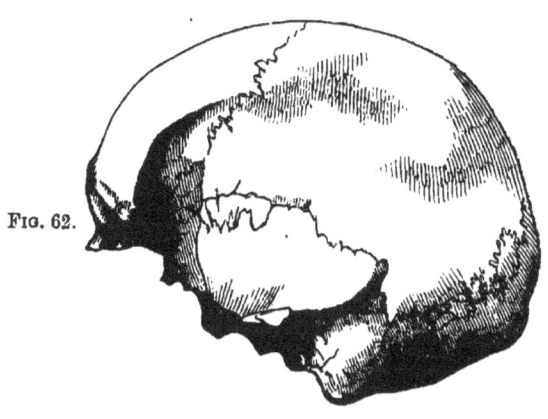

Fig. 62.

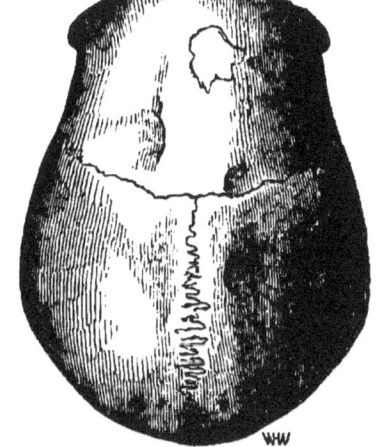

Fig. 63.

Fig. 62.—*Norma lateralis.*   Fig. 63.—*Norma verticalis.*

The Australian Skull.

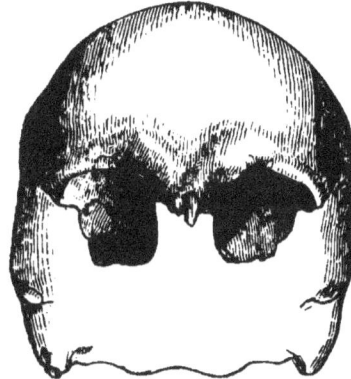

Fig. 64.

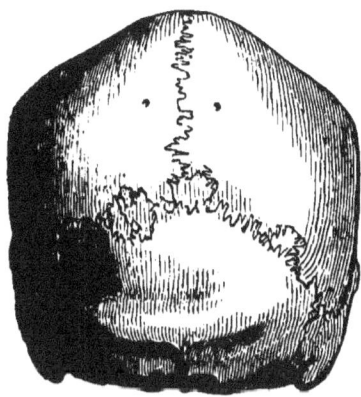

Fig. 65.

Fig. 64.—*Norma frontalis.*   Fig. 65.—*Norma occipitalis.*

APPENDIX.

NOTE A.

THE volume of "Memoirs read before the Anthropological Society," for 1863-4, contains a paper by Dr. J. B. Davis, entitled "The Neanderthal Skull; its peculiar conformation explained anatomically." The insufficiency of the "explanation" thus offered by Dr. Davis, was, immediately afterwards, clearly demonstrated by Dr. Thurnam—to whose valuable memoir, "On Synostosis of the Cranial bones," published in the "Natural History Review," for April, 1865, I may refer those who are desirous to learn the conditions under which, alone, the doctrine of synostosis is applicable to the explanation of cranial peculiarities. Nevertheless, as I find that Dr. Davis' "explanation" is still quoted as all-sufficient, to the delusion of those who are unable to examine the matter for themselves, I will say a few words upon the subject here; though, really, after Dr. Thurnam's paper, controversion of the "synostotic" explanation is as much a work of supererogation as would be that of the "idiotic" hypothesis, which was so long held by other instructors of the public.

Dr. Davis' views are thus stated by himself: (*l.c.* p. 286)

"In the application of these remarks to the famous Neanderthal calvarium, the first striking peculiarity that demands attention is the great magnitude of the frontal sinuses, and the enormous ridge of bone covering them, which are not affected by irregularity in the ossification of sutures. The size of these sinuses differs greatly in different persons, and to have them remarkably large is merely an individual peculiarity. Some living persons among Englishmen might be brought forward exhibiting this peculiarity.(1) And in the example figured, No. 1029, the same peculiarity will be seen to exist. (2) Still it should be remarked that the unusual depression of the frontal bone above the superciliary ridges gives an exaggerated prominence to this part of the Neanderthal calvarium. (3) This depression, only slightly diminished in degree, will be seen in the example figured. The fact of its being less is at once explained by the open state of the sutures surrounding the alisphenoid, all of which appear to have been prematurely ossified in the Neanderthal skull.(4)

"It is precisely this early synostosis of the bones forming the temporal regions that has prevented the development and arching of the frontal bone, and given rise to the *great* depression and flatness of this bone, one of the most remarkable features of the Neanderthal calvarium.*(5) Indeed, it is the enormous superciliary ridge and the depressed forehead which have led so many excellent observers to the verge of a declination towards pithecoid forms.(6) In these particulars, and in the great gap separating it from the body of the frontal bone, the Neanderthal calvaria may be said at first view to be suggestive of the crest of the gorilla. But there is no real resemblance between the two; for the latter crest is a solid buttress of bone, and does not correspond to the hollow superciliary ridge.(7) It will thus be seen that there is nothing either of a simious character, or that might not have been expected in the low forehead of the Neanderthal skull, in which the brain had to grow and expand under a plate of bone which appears to have been, in a great degree, in one solid piece. It was impossible to raise this

---

* "That is, in addition to the ossification of the coronal suture," Dr. Davis adds in a note.

plate of bone upwards, and the result, as will be seen, was a development in another direction. In the middle region of the calvaria, the sagittal suture being closed, the contained cerebral substance could only expand at the sides in the situation of the squamous sutures; and here the Neanderthal cranium seems not to lack development. (8) But in the posterior region its greatest expansion took place, precisely because in this part was the open lambdoidal suture, which admitted of the growth of the brain. In the figures of this imperfect calvarium the superior occipital scale is seen to be bulged out, and the whole of what remains of the occipital bone is full and large—the compensatory result for the contracted anterior regions.

"The extreme length of the Neanderthal cranium is given by Professor Huxley, and is eight inches, which is a very unusual length. In skulls in which such a length occurs it is most frequently the result of synostosis. That such is the case in the Neanderthal example there is not any doubt. This feature is the unequivocal effect of premature ossification of longitudinal sutures." (9)

Upon these statements I have to offer the following remarks :—

(1) We all know that the large size of the frontal sinuses is very often merely an individual peculiarity. But the, question is, whether frontal sinuses and supraciliary ridges, so large as those of the Neanderthal skull, are known in any other human skull. I have ventured to answer that question in the negative, and Dr. Davis produces not a tittle of evidence against the justice of that negation.

(2) If the figure at p. 288, of the work cited, is a correct representation of the skull 1029, nothing like "the same peculiarity" exists in it. In fact, the form of the skull in question is nowise more remarkable than that of the *Batavus*

genuinus of Blumenbach, a figure of which, compared with

FIG. 66.

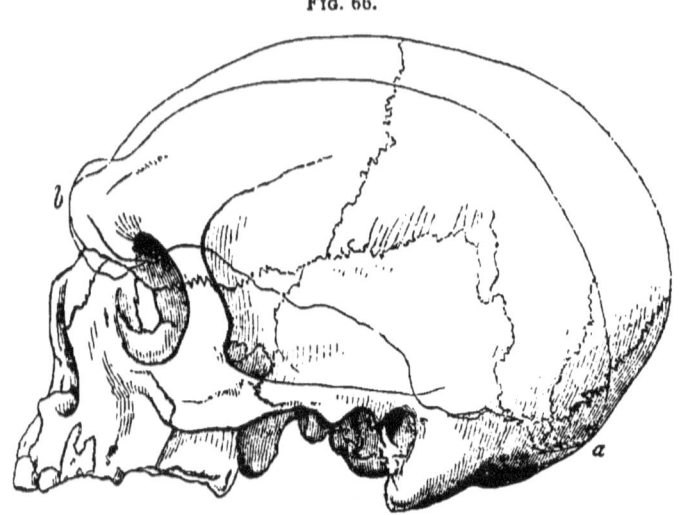

Reduced copy of Blumenbach's figure of a "Batavus genuinus." The contour of the Neanderthal skull, reduced to the same length, is drawn upon the figure; the glabellæ being made to correspond, and the superior curved line of the Neanderthal skull being adjusted to the point *a* of the other. The skulls are not reduced to the same scale, and hence this figure only gives the different proportions of the two.

that of the Neanderthal skull, I have already given ("Natural History Review," July, 1864), and here reproduce (fig. 66).

(3) Exactly the reverse is the case, as will be seen by comparing the casts of the inner cavities of the Australian and the Neanderthal skulls (fig. 67). It is not the frontal contour of the Neanderthal skull which really differs so much from that of ordinary skulls; but it is the enormous development of the supraciliary ridges which make that contour look more retreating than it really is.

(4) How does Dr. Davis know what was the condition of the sutures "surrounding the alisphenoid" in the Neanderthal skull? No observer who has seen the skull says a word

about either the alispheno-frontal, or the alispheno-parietal, sutures. Dr. Fuhlrott is cited by Dr. Davis, as saying, "5. Of all *the other sutures*, namely, those taking their course on the points of examination, on the frontal, parietal, and squamosal bones there is nothing to be found, even no partial indication 'einseitige Andentung.'" I cannot but think that Dr. Fuhlrott's words have here been "overset," as his countrymen would say, into English—for in their Anglican dress they are not very intelligible, though I have reason to know that Dr. Fuhlrott expresses himself with much clearness in his native tongue and in French. For my own part, I venture very greatly to doubt that the region which should exhibit the alispheno-frontal and alispheno-parietal sutures is preserved in the Neanderthal calvaria. And if this be the case, while Dr. Fuhlrott may very properly speak of the absence of the sutures, it is surely not very proper for anyone else to confound the absence of a suture, in virtue of the absence of the part of the skull which should show it, with its obliteration by synostosis. Furthermore, if alisphenoidal synostosis is the cause of the frontal depression of the Neanderthal skull, why is that depression "only slightly diminished in degree" in the skull 1029, in which the "sutures surroundding the alisphenoid" are in an "open state"? It is surely odd to find an effect "only slightly diminished," when the cause of that effect is absent.

(5) The "synostotic" hypothesis is apparently cumulative in its effect on those who hold it. Two or three lines above, Dr. Davis was content with "premature" alisphenoidal synostosis, now he assumes "early synostosis of the bones forming the temporal regions." But, the temporal bones themselves take a certain, not inconsiderable, share in "forming the temporal regions;" and yet Dr. Fuhlrott, as quoted by Dr. Davis, tells us, "of the squamous suture, the middle portions on both sides of the skull, are obviously present upon the pa-

rietal bone." Surely Dr. Davis has not again taken Dr. Fuhlrott's silence touching that part of the skull which is absent for evidence of more synostosis? But if he has not, on what ground does he assert that such synostosis exists? And furthermore, 'supposing any synostosis to exist in the temporal region, what shadow of evidence is there that it took place early? The Neanderthal skull, judging from the great development of the frontal sinuses and other marks, is that of a man verging on, if he were not in, the middle period of life; and we have no means of judging at what time any of its sutures closed. But, on this point I refer the reader to the excellent criticism of Dr. Thurnam.

(6) Which of us has been brought to this pass? I have not the pleasure of knowing Dr. Fuhlrott, or Professor Schaafhausen, Professor King, or Dr. Davis, personally, but I have noted no sign approaching even "the verge of such declination towards pithecoid forms" in either Mr. Busk, Mr. Turner, or myself, though such a phenomenon would certainly attract my attention strongly; and would, indeed, be a notable judgment upon such of us as may be believers in progressive modification, convicted, henceforth, rather of retrogression. *Absit omen!*

(7) Why does Dr. Davis venture broad statements about matters concerning which he is not well informed; especially when those statements have already been refuted? In replying to Professor Mayer, who fell into the same error as Dr. Davis, I have already affirmed ("Natural History Review," July, 1864) : "There are to be seen, at the present moment, in the Museum of the Royal College of Surgeons, two bisected skulls, one of a gorilla and one of a chimpanzee, in which the frontal sinuses are enormous, their walls being no thicker, in proportion, than in man." I ask no one to take this, or anything else, for granted, on my authority; but surely my assertion might have furnished Dr. Davis with

some *primâ facie* inducement to look at the skulls to which I refer, and submit to their authority.

(8) But if "the early synostosis of the bones forming the temporal regions prevented the development and arching of the frontal bone" in the Neanderthal cranium, surely it must have no less prevented expansion at the sides, in the situation of the squamous sutures. By Dr. Davis' hypothesis, the premature synostosis of the sagittal suture prevented the brain from growing in width under the parietal bones; in what way, then, could it have developed in the region of the squamous suture without dislocating the squamosals from the parietals?

(9) By way of reply to all this I reproduce a figure which I

Fig. 67.

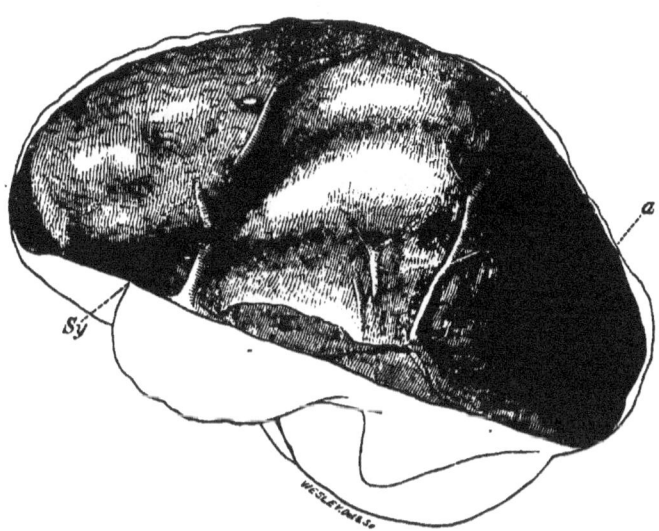

Side view of the cast of the interior of the Neanderthal skull reduced to one half of the natural size. The outline represents the contour of a like cast of an Australian skull in the Museum of the Royal College of Surgeons (No. 5331) reduced to the same scale. *a*. Cast of the inner face of the lambdoidal suture. *Sy*. the Sylvian fissure.

published in the paper in the "Natural History Review," for

1864, already cited, exhibiting the interior casts of the Neanderthal skull and that of an Australian skull (No. 5331 in the

FIG. 68.

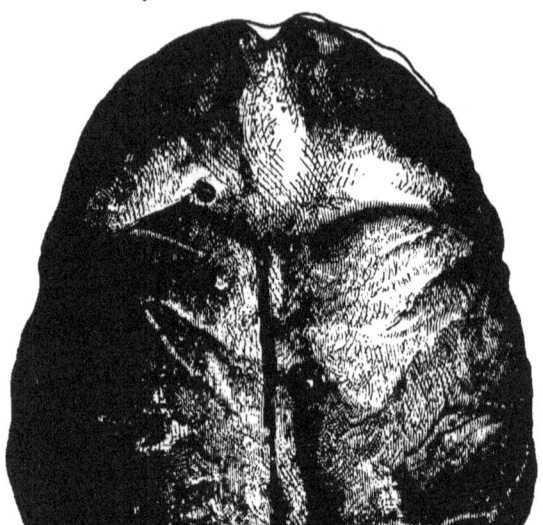

Represents the same objects as Fig. 67, viewed from above; scale the same. *a a.* as before.

Museum of the Royal College of Surgeons). What is essential about the form of a skull is the form of its interior; the external skull may be modified in many adventitious ways, when the interior, which corresponds with the form of the brain, is once completely moulded.

It will be observed that these casts correspond so closely that their differences are insignificant. On the whole, the Australian is absolutely longer than the Neanderthal (7.1 in. to 6.85 in.) and absolutely narrower (5.3 in. to 5.45 in.);

and, furthermore, the protuberance of the occipital lobes is more marked and more sharply defined in the Australian skull. In point of depression of the frontal region the Neanderthal cast slightly exceeds the Australian, but the depression of the parietal lobes is equal in the two. But whatever other peculiarity the Neanderthal brain had, the Australian brain had in a greater degree; and if these peculiarities are due to synostosis in the Neanderthal skull, there ought to be as much, or more, synostosis in the Australian.

What are the facts? In the Australian skull every suture of the calvaria normally present in an adult skull, viz., the coronal, sagittal, lambdoidal, occipito-mastoid, squamosal, alisphenoidal, is open; not one showing the smallest sign of obliteration. Would it not have been worth Dr. Davis' while (as he has read the paper from which he has done me the honour to quote a phrase) to have looked at No. 5331, as well as at the gorilla skull, in the College Museum, before he undertook to "explain the Neanderthal skull anatomically"?

NOTE B.

M. BROCA, in his very able and instructive paper "Sur l'Ethnologie de la France" (Mémoires de la Societé d'Anthropologie de Paris, i., 1860), thus sums up the views adopted by M. W. Edwards and himself.

"The Celtic and the Kymric races are certainly the two chief sources of the French people. In the midst of our variously-mixed populations, M. W. Edwards was able to discover the principal distinctive characters of these two great Gaulish races. The Gaels (Galls) or Celts, properly so called, had a middle stature, the forehead arched, receding towards the temples, the nose nearly straight and ending in a rounded lobule, the chin round, *the head round*. The

Kymry, or Belgæ of Cæsar, had a much greater stature: *their heads were long*, the forehead wide and high, the chin projecting and strongly marked, the nose curved, with the point directed downwards, and its alæ raised laterally. I add, to complete the contrast, that the Celts had their hair and eyes brown, or black, while the Kymry had the eyes light and the hair blonde" (*l.c.* p. 8).

And in another place, in describing the remarkable differences between the Kymric colony of Léon in Brittany, and the Gaelic inhabitants of the adjacent "pays de Cornuaille," M. Broca states, on the authority of a correspondent, familiar with the country, that the people of Léon are very tall, blonde, light-eyed, with *long heads*, long noses, pointed chins, and very fair skins. The inhabitants of Cornuaille, on the other hand, are short, dark complexioned, and with dark hair and eyes, *round heads*, and round chins (*l.c.* p. 21). At the same time, M. Broca identifies the "Celts" of Cornuaille with those of Ireland (*l.c.* p. 24), and the Kymri of Léon with the Belgæ of Southern England (*l.c.* p. 20).

Thus M. Broca exactly reverses the conclusions of Dr. Thurnam. But it is to be remarked—

Firstly: that M. Broca's conclusions do not seem to be based upon measurements.

Secondly: that the Irish "Celts," with whom he identifies the French "Celts," are certainly not a round-headed people.

Thirdly: that Dr. Thurnam's position, that the broad-headed people of Southern England were Belgæ, and consequently identical with the French Kymri, is very strong; and that, in any case, the broad-headed people were the only tall ancient people of Southern England.

Fourthly: that Professor Wilson has recently brought forward some curious indirect evidence which tells in exactly the same direction, in his "Inquiry into the physical characteristics of the ancient and modern Celt of Gaul and Britain."*

In Lower Canada, according to this careful investigator, the French inhabitants of Quebec are derived, almost wholly, from Normandy; while those of Montreal, on the other hand, are a colony from Brittany. On examining the patterns of the heads of Canadians taken by hatters, with an instrument termed the "conformateur," Prof. Wilson found, that of nearly 100 Quebec French skulls, only nine were other than oval and nearly round. On the other hand, the Montreal French heads were almost all elongated. Now a great part of Normandy was included in Belgic Gaul, and M. Broca brings forward evidence to prove that, in their stature, its population shows clear evidence of the influence of Belgic blood, and is very sharply marked off from the closely adjacent Brittany.

I cannot support the view to which Professor Wilson seems inclined, that among the Norsemen of historical times there was any notable infusion of Finnic elements: all the information we possess respecting the old Scandinavian invaders being, I think, adverse to such an opinion. But if the Norsemen were all, as I believe they were, long-skulled, and the Franks who preceded them in Normandy were also dolichocephalic (as they certainly were) the brachycephaly of the Norman-French colonists of Quebec, can only come from their atavic ancestors, the Belgæ.

In like manner, the dolichocephaly of the Breton colonists of Montreal is dead against the notion that the French "Celts" are broad-headed, but in perfect accordance with what we know of the short and dark-haired population of the British Islands. I have yet to meet with good evidence, in favour of the existence, in Europe, of any short, dark,

* "The Canadian Journal," 1864.

brachycephalic people, except the Lapps; or of any tall, fair *brachycephali*, except the short-headed *Xanthochroi*, who, in different regions, have passed, or pass, under the names of Slavonians, Fins, Belgæ, South Germans, or Swiss. From time immemorial, these people have spoken Slavonic dialects in the centre of their area; while, at its margin, they have been, and are, found using those of the nations with whom they came into contact: Celtic, and afterwards French, in Gaul; Ugrian, in Finmark; German, Romance, or French, in Switzerland and Germany; Latin, in Italy; modern Greek, in Greece.

	1. Straight Lines.												2. Curved Lines.									3. Proportions (length taken as 1.00).	
	1. Length.	2. Breadth.	3. Height.	4. Greatest frontal breadth.	5. Parietal breadth.	6. Occipital breadth.	7. Zygomatic breadth.	8. Frontal radius.	9. Vertical radius.	10. Parietal radius.	11. Occipital radius.	12. Maxillary radius.	13. Circumference.	14. Longitudinal arc.	15. Longitudinal frontal.	16. Longitudinal parietal.	17. Longitudinal occipital.	18. Frontal transverse arc.	19. Vertical transverse arc.	20. Parietal transverse arc.	21. Occipital transverse arc.	22. Of breadth.	23. Of height.
No. 7....	7.45	5.85	5.3	5	5.75	4.5	5.0	4.7	4.75	5.0	4.1	3.85	21.5	15.85	5.5	4.95	5.4?	12.2	13	13.6	11	.78	.71
No. 8....	7.5	5.7	5.45	4.8	5.65	4.4	...	4.5	4.65	4.85	4.0	...	21	14.9	5.3	5.0	4.6	12	12.4	13.5	10.4	.76	.73
No. 2....	6.9	5.4	5.1	4.3	5.3	4.55	5.0	4.16	4.35	4.7	3.8	3.5	20	13.0	4.5	4.9	4.5	11.2	12	12.75	9.6	.78	.74
No. 1....	7.25	5.3	4.7	4.05	5.3	4.4	5.0	4.15	4.15	4.7	4.15	3.95	20.2	13.8	4.5	4.9	4.4	11	11.5	12.7	10.6	.73	.65
No. 3....	7.0	5.3	4.9	4.4	5.15	4.15	5.0	4.55	4.6	4.65	3.8	3.75	19.6	14.5	4.95	4.7	4.7	11.3	12.3	12.5	9.7	.76	.70
No. 5....	7.2	5.45	5.?	4.5	6.1	4.2	...	4.3	4.45	4.7	4.3	3.55	20.3	14.8	6.0	5.3	4.5	11.35	12.35	12.7	10.7	.75	.70
No. 9.*..	7.2	5.1	5.2	4.3	5	4.3	4.75	4.3	4.7	4.85	4.3	3.7	20.3	14.7	4.8	5.0	4.9	11.6	12.0	13.2	10.6	.70	.72

1. Length from glabellum to extreme point of occiput.
2. Breadth—extreme.
3. Height—greatest distance from level of anterior and posterior margin of foramen magnum to vertex.
4. Breadth of frontal where the temporal line crosses the coronal suture.
5. Breadth of parietal where the temporal line passes over the parietal protuberance.
6. Breadth of occipital.
7. Breadth between the zygomatic arches.
8. Radius of frontal, measured from the middle of auditory foramen (not the arch).
9. Radius of vertical.
10. Radius of parietal, measured from middle of auditory foramen to highest part of parietal.
11. Radius of occipital, measured from middle of auditory foramen to most distant part of occipital.
12. Radius of maxillary.
13. Circumference—greatest.
14. Longitudinal arc, divided into—
15. Longitudinal arc of os frontis.
16. Longitudinal arc of parietal.
17. Longitudinal arc of occipital.
18. Transverse arc of frontal, measured from middle of foramen auditorium to middle line of frontal over the protuberance, and doubled.
19. Transverse arc of vertical.
20. Transverse arc of parietal, from same point over middle of parietal to opposite side.
21. Transverse arc of occipital, from same point to summit of os occipitis.
22. Proportion of breadth to length—the latter regarded as = 1.00.
23. Proportion of height to length—the latter regarded as = 1.00.

* (Mr. Turner's)

HERTFORD:
PRINTED BY STEPHEN AUSTIN.

14, HENRIETTA STREET, COVENT GARDEN, LONDON;
20, SOUTH FREDERICK STREET, EDINBURGH.

CATALOGUE OF SOME WORKS

PUBLISHED BY

WILLIAMS & NORGATE.

Agnostic's Progress, An, from the Known to the Unknown. 268 pp. Crown 8vo, cloth. 5s.

Alviella (Count Goblet d') The Contemporary Evolution of Religious Thought in England, America and India. Translated by J. MODEN. 8vo, cloth. 10s. 6d.

Baur (F. C.) Church History of the First Three Centuries. Translated from the Third German Edition. Edited by the Rev. ALLAN MENZIES. 2 vols. 8vo. 21s.
— Vide Theological Translation Fund Library.

Baur (F. C.) Paul, the Apostle of Jesus Christ, his Life and Work, his Epistles and his Doctrine. A Contribution to the Critical History of Primitive Christianity. Edited by E. ZELLER. Translated by Rev. ALLAN MENZIES. 2 vols. 8vo, cloth. 21s.
— Vide Theological Translation Fund Library.

Beard (Rev. Chas.) Lectures on the Reformation of the Sixteenth Century in its Relation to Modern Thought and Knowledge. Hibbert Lectures, 1883. 8vo, cloth. [Cheap Edition, 4s. 6d.] 10s. 6d.

Beard (Rev. Chas.) Port Royal, a Contribution to the History of Religion and Literature in France. Cheaper Edition. 2 vols. Crown 8vo. 12s.

Beard (Rev. Dr. J. R.) The Autobiography of Satan. Crown 8vo, cloth. 7s. 6d.

Bible for Young People. A Critical, Historical, and Moral Handbook to the Old and New Testaments. By Dr. H. OORT and Dr. J. HOOYKAAS, with the assistance of Dr. KUENEN. Translated from the Dutch by the Rev. P. H. WICKSTEED. Vols. I. to IV., Old Testament, 12s.; V. VI., New Testament, 8s. Maps. 6 vols. Crown 8vo, cloth. 20s.

Bleek (F.) Lectures on the Apocalypse. Edited by T. HOSSBACH. Edited by the Rev. Dr. S. DAVIDSON. 8vo, cloth. 10s. 6d.
— Vide Theological Translation Fund Library.

Channing's Complete Works, including the "Perfect Life," with
a brief Memoir. Centenary Edition. 868 pp. Crown 8vo, 1s.; cloth, 2s.
—— The same, large type, 4to, cloth. 7s. 6d.

Cobbe (Miss F. P.) The Hopes of the Human Race, Hereafter and
Here. Essays on the Life after Death. With a Preface having special
reference to Mr. Mill's Essay on Religion. Second Edition. Crown 8vo,
cloth. 5s.

Cobbe (Miss F. P.) Darwinism in Morals, and (13) other Essays
(Religion in Childhood, Unconscious Cerebration, Dreams, the Devil, Auricular
Confession, &c. &c.). 400 pp. 8vo, cloth. (pub. at 10s.) 5s.

Cobbe (Miss F. P.) The Duties of Women. A Course of Lectures
delivered in London and Clifton. Second Edition. Crown 8vo, cloth. 5s.

Cobbe (Miss F. P.) The Peak in Darien, and other Riddles of Life
and Death. Crown 8vo, cloth. 7s. 6d.

Cobbe (Miss F. P.) A Faithless World. With Additions and a
Preface. 8vo, cloth. 2s. 6d.

Cobbe (Miss F. P.) Broken Lights. An Inquiry into the Present
Condition and Future Prospects of Religious Faith. Third Edition. Crown
8vo, cloth. 5s.

Cobbe (Miss F. P.) Dawning Lights. An Inquiry concerning the
Secular Results of the New Reformation. 8vo, cloth. 5s.

Cobbe (Miss F. P.) Alone to the Alone. Prayers for Theists, by
several Contributors. Third Edition. Crown 8vo, cloth, gilt edges. 5s.

Davids (T. W. Rhys) Lectures on the Origin and Growth of Religion, as illustrated by some Points in the History of Indian Buddhism.
Hibbert Lectures, 1881. 8vo, cloth. 10s. 6d.

Echoes of Holy Thoughts: arranged as Private Meditations before
a First Communion. Second Edition, with a Preface by the Rev. J. HAMILTON THOM, of Liverpool. Printed with red lines. Crown 8vo, cloth. 2s. 6d.

Evolution of Christianity, The. By CHARLES GILL. Second Edition,
with Dissertations in answer to Criticism. 8vo, cloth. 12s.

Ewald (Professor H.) Commentary on the Prophets of the Old Testament. Translated by the Rev. J. FRED. SMITH. Vol. I. Yoel, Amos,
Hozea, and Zakharya ix.—xi. Vol. II. Yesayah, Obadya, Micah. Vol. III.
Nahum, Sephanya, Habaqquq, Zakharya xii.—xiv., Yeremiah. Vol. IV.
Hezekiel, Yesaya xl.—lxvi., with Translation. Vol. V. Haggai, Zakharya,
Malaki, Jona, Baruch, Appendix and Index. Complete in 5 vols. 8vo,
cloth. each 10s. 6d.
—— Vide Theological Translation Fund Library.

**Ewald (Professor H.) Commentary on the Psalms. (Poetical Books
of the Old Testament. Part I.)** Translated by the Rev. E. JOHNSON, M.A.
2 vols. 8vo, cloth. each 10s. 6d.
— Vide Theological Translation Fund Library.

**Ewald (Professor H.) Commentary on the Book of Job. (Poetical
Books, Part II.)** Translated by the Rev. J. FREDERICK SMITH. 8vo,
cloth. 10s. 6d.
— Vide Theological Translation Fund Library.

Gould (S. Baring) Lost and Hostile Gospels. An Account of the
Toledoth Jesher, two Hebrew Gospels circulating in the Middle Ages, and
extant Fragments of the Gospels of the First Three Centuries of Petrine and
Pauline Origin. By the Rev. S. BARING GOULD. Crown 8vo, cloth. 7s. 6d.

**Hanson (Sir Richard) The Apostle Paul and the Preaching of
Christianity in the Primitive Church.** By Sir RICHARD DAVIS HANSON,
Chief Justice of South Australia, Author of "The Jesus of History," "Letters
to and from Rome," &c. 8vo, cloth. (pub. at 12s.) 7s. 6d.

**Hausrath. History of the New Testament Times. The Time of
Jesus.** By Dr. A. HAUSRATH, Professor of Theology, Heidelberg. Translated,
with the Author's sanction, from the Second German Edition, by the Revds.
C. T. POYNTING and P. QUENZER. 2 vols. 8vo, cloth. 21s.
— Vide Theological Translation Fund Library.

Hibbert Lectures, vide Beard, Davids, Kuenen, Müller, Pfleiderer,
Renan, Renouf, Reville, Rhys.

Horne (Rev. W.) Religious Life and Thought. By WILLIAM
HORNE, M.A., Dundee, Examiner in Philosophy in the University of St.
Andrews; Author of "Reason and Revelation." Crown 8vo, cloth. 3s. 6d.

**Jones (Rev. R. Crompton) Hymns of Duty and Faith, selected and
arranged.** Second Edition. 247 pp. Foolscap 8vo, cloth. 3s. 6d.

**Jones (Rev. R. Crompton) Psalms and Canticles, selected and
pointed for Chanting.** 18mo, cloth. 1s. 6d.
— Anthems, with Indexes and References to the Music. 18mo, cloth. 1s. 3d.
— The Chants and Anthems, together in 1 vol. 2s. 6d.
— A Book of Prayer in 30 Orders of Worship, for Public or Private Devotions.
12mo, cloth, 2s. 6d.
— The same with the Chants. 18mo, cloth. 3s.

**Keim's History of Jesus of Nazara, considered in its connection
with the National Life of Israel, and related in detail.** Translated from the
German by A. RANSOM and the Rev. E. M. GELDART, in 6 vols. 8vo,
cloth. each 10s. 6d.
— Vide Theological Translation Fund Library.

Knighton (W.) Struggles for Life. By WILLIAM KNIGHTON, LL.D.
Vice-President of the Royal Society of Literature; Author of "The History
of Ceylon," "Forest Life in Ceylon," &c. &c. 8vo, cloth. 10s. 6d

Kuenen (Dr. A.) The Religion of Israel to the Fall of the Jewish
State. By Dr. A. KUENEN, Professor of Theology at the University, Leyden
Translated from the Dutch by A. H. MAY. 3 vols. 8vo, cloth. 31s. 6d
—— Vide Theological Translation Fund Library.

Kuenen (Professor A.) Lectures on National Religions and Universal Religions. Delivered in Oxford and London. By A. KUENEN, LL.D., D.D.
Professor of Theology at Leyden. Hibbert Lectures, 1882. 10s. 6d

Macan (Reg. W.) The Resurrection of Jesus Christ. An Essay
in Three Chapters. Published for the Hibbert Trustees. 8vo, cloth. 5s

Mackay (R. W.) Sketch of the Rise and Progress of Christianity
8vo, cloth. (pub. at 10s. 6d.) 6s

Martineau (Rev. Dr. James) Religion as affected by Modern Materialism; and, Modern Materialism: its Attitude towards Theology. A Critique
and Defence. 8vo. 2s. 6d
—— The Relation between Ethics and Religion. 8vo. 1s
—— Ideal Substitutes for God considered. 8vo. 1s

Mind: a Quarterly Review of Psychology and Philosophy. Contributions by Mr. Herbert Spencer, Professor Bain, Mr. Henry Sidgwick
Mr. Shadworth H. Hodgson, Professor Flint, Mr. James Sully, the Rev. John
Venn, the Editor (Professor Croom Robertson), and others. Vols. I. to XI.
1876 to 1886, each 12s.; cloth, 13s. 6d. 12s. per annum, post free

Müller (Professor Max) Lectures on the Origin and Growth o
Religion, as illustrated by the Religions of India. Hibbert Lectures, 1878
8vo, cloth. 10s. 6d

Oldenberg (Prof. H.) Buddha: his Life, his Doctrine, his Order
Translated by WILLIAM HOEY, M.A., D.Lit., Member of the Royal Asiati
Society, Asiatic Society of Bengal, &c., of her Majesty's Bengal Civil Service
Cloth, gilt. 18s

Peill (Rev. G.) The Three-fold Basis of Universal Restitution
Crown 8vo, cloth. 3s

Pfleiderer (O.) Paulinism. An Essay towards the History of the
Theology of Primitive Christianity. Translated by E. PETERS, Esq. 2 vols
8vo, cloth. 21s
—— Vide Theological Translation Fund Library.

Pfleiderer (Professor O.) The Philosophy of Religion on the Basis
of its History. I. History of the Philosophy of Religion from Spinoza to
the present Day. Vol. I. Spinoza to Schleiermacher. By Professor OTTO
PFLEIDERER. Translated by the Rev. ALLAN MENZIES and the Rev. ALEX
STEWART, of Dundee. 8vo, cloth. 10s. 6d
—— Vide Theological Translation Fund Library.

Pfleiderer (Professor O.) Lectures on the Influence of the Apostle Paul on the Development of Christianity. Translated by the Rev. J. FREDERICK SMITH. Hibbert Lectures, 1885. 8vo, cloth. 10s. 6d.

Poole (Reg. Lane) Illustrations of the History of Medieval Thought, in the Departments of Theology and Ecclesiastical Politics. 8vo, cloth. 10s. 6d.

Pratt (Dr. H.) New Aspects of Life and Religion. 440 pp. Crown 8vo, cloth. 7s. 6d.

Protestant Commentary, A Short, on the New Testament, with General and Special Introductions. From the German of Hilgenfeld, Holtzmann, Lang, Pfleiderer, Lipsius, and others. Translated by the Rev. F. H. JONES, of Oldham. 3 vols. 8vo, cloth. each 10s. 6d.
—— Vide Theological Translation Fund Library.

Renan (E.) On the Influence of the Institutions, Thought and Culture of Rome on Christianity, and the Development of the Catholic Church. By ERNEST RENAN, Membre de l'Institute. Translated by the Rev. CHARLES BEARD, of Liverpool. Hibbert Lectures, 1880. 8vo, cloth. [Cheap Edition, 2s. 6d.] 10s. 6d.

Renouf (P. Le Page) Lectures on the Origin and Growth of Religion, as illustrated by the Religion of Ancient Egypt. Hibbert Lectures, 1879. 8vo, cloth. 10s. 6d.

Reville (Prof. Albert) Prolegomena of the History of Religions. By ALBERT REVILLE, D.D., Professor in the Collége de France, and Hibbert Lecturer, 1884. Translated from the French. With an Introduction by Professor F. MAX MÜLLER. 8vo, cloth. 10s. 6d.
—— Vide Theological Translation Fund Library.

Reville (Prof. Albert) Lectures on the Origin and Growth of Religion, as illustrated by the Native Religions of Mexico and Peru. Translated by the Rev. P. H. WICKSTEED, M.A. Hibbert Lectures, 1884. 8vo, cl. 10s. 6d.

Reville (Rev. Dr. A.) The Song of Songs, commonly called the Song of Solomon, or the Canticle. Crown 8vo, cloth. 1s. 6d.

Reville (Rev. Dr. A.) The Devil: his Origin, Greatness, and Decadence. Translated from the French. Second Edition. 12mo, cloth. 2s.

Rhys (Professor J.) Lectures on the Origin and Growth of Religion as illustrated by Celtic Heathendom. Hibbert Lectures, 1886. 8vo, cl. 10s. 6d.

Samuelson (Jas.) Views of the Deity, Traditional and Scientific; a Contribution to the Study of Theological Science. By JAMES SAMUELSON, Esq., of the Middle Temple, Barrister-at-law, Founder and former Editor of the Quarterly Journal of Science. Crown 8vo, cloth. 4s. 6d.

Savage (Rev. M. J.) Beliefs about the Bible. By the Rev. M. J. SAVAGE, of the Unity Church, Boston, Mass., Author of "Belief in God," "Beliefs about Man," &c. &c. 8vo, cloth. 7s. 6d.

Schurman (J. G.) Kantian Ethics and the Ethics of Evolution. A
Critical Study, by J. GOULD SCHURMAN, M.A. D.Sc., Professor of Logic and
Metaphysics in Acadia College, Nova Scotia. Published by the Hibbert
Trustees. 8vo, cloth. 5s.

Seth (A.) The Development from Kant to Hegel, with Chapters on
the Philosophy of Religion. By ANDREW SETH, Assistant to the Professor of
Logic and Metaphysics, Edinburgh University. Published by the Hibbert
Trustees. 8vo, cloth. 5s.

Sharpe (S.) History of the Hebrew Nation and its Literature, with
an Appendix on the Hebrew Chronology. Fourth Edition. 487 pp. 8vo,
cloth. 7s. 6d.

Sharpe (S.) Bible. The Holy Bible, translated by SAMUEL SHARPE,
being a Revision of the Authorized English Version. Fourth Edition of the
Old Testament; Eighth Edition of the New Testament. 8vo, roan. 4s. 6d.

Sharpe (S.) The New Testament. Translated from Griesbach's
Text. 14th Thousand, fcap. 8vo, cloth. 1s. 6d

Smith (Rev. J. Fred.) Studies in Religion under German Masters.
Essays on Herder, Goethe, Lessing, Franck, and Lang. By the Rev. J. FRE
DERICK SMITH, of Mansfield. Crown 8vo, cloth. 5s

Spencer (Herbert) Works. The Doctrine of Evolution. 8vo, cloth
First Principles. Sixth Thousand. 16s
Principles of Biology. 2 vols. 34s
Principles of Psychology. Fourth Thousand. 2 vols. 36s
Principles of Sociology. Vol. I. 21s
Ceremonial Institutions. Principles of Sociology. Vol. II. Part I. 7s
Political Institutions. Principles of Sociology. Vol. II. Part II. 12s
The Data of Ethics. Principles of Morality. Fourth Thousand. Part I. 8s

Spencer (Herbert) The Study of Sociology. Library Edition (being
the Ninth), with a Postscript. 8vo, cloth. 10s. 6c
—— Education (Cheap Edition, Seventh Thousand, 2s. 6d.). 6.
—— Essays. 2 vols. Third Edition. 16.
—— Essays (Third Series). Third Edition. 8

Spencer (Herbert) The Man *versus* the State. 1s.; or on bette
paper, in cloth, 2s. 6c

Spencer (Herbert) The Philosophy of M. Comte—Reasons for Dis
senting from it. (Republished from "The Classification of the Sciences," &c
1864.) 6c

Spinoza. Four Essays, by Professors J. LAND, KUNO FISCHER, an
VAN VLOTEN, and ERNEST RENAN. Edited, with an Introduction, by Pro
fessor W. KNIGHT, of St. Andrews. 8vo, cloth. 5

Stokes (G. J.) The Objectivity of Truth. By GEORGE J. STOKES,
B.A., Senior Moderator and Gold Medallist, Trinity College, Dublin; late
Hibbert Travelling Scholar. Published by the Hibbert Trustees. 8vo, cloth. 5s.

Strauss (Dr. D. F.) New Life of Jesus, for the People. The
Authorized English Edition. 2 vols. 8vo, cloth. 24s.

Tayler (Rev. J. J.) An Attempt to ascertain the Character of the
Fourth Gospel, especially in its Relation to the First Three. New Edition,
8vo, cloth. 5s.

Ten Services of Public Prayer, taken in Substance from the "Common Prayer for Christian Worship," with a few additional Prayers for particular Days.
> Ten Services alone, crown 8vo, cloth, 2s. 6d.; with Special Collects. 3s.
> Ten Services alone, 32mo, 1s.; with Special Collects. 1s. 6d.
> Psalms and Canticles. (To accompany the same.) Crown 8vo, 1s. 6d.
> With Anthems. 2s.

Thoughts for Every Day in the Year. Selected from the Writings
of Spiritually-minded Persons. By the Author of "Visiting my Relations."
Printed within red lines. Crown 8vo, cloth. 2s. 6d.

Theological Translation Fund. A Series of Translations, by which
the best results of recent Theological investigations on the Continent, conducted without reference to doctrinal considerations, and with the sole purpose of arriving at truth, will be placed within reach of English readers. A literature which is represented by such works as those of Ewald, F. C. Baur, Zeller, Roth, Keim, Nöldeke, &c., in Germany, and by those of Kuenen, Scholten and others in Holland.

> *Three* Volumes annually for *a Guinea* Subscription. The Prospectus, bearing the signatures of Principal Tulloch, Dean Stanley, Professors Jowett, H. J. Smith, Henry Sidgwick, the Rev. Dr. Martineau, Mr. W. G. Clark, the Rev. T. K. Cheyne, Principal Caird and others, may be had.

36 *Volumes published* (1873 to 1886) *for* £12. 12s.
Protestant Commentary, a Short, on the New Testament. 3 vols.
Keim's History of Jesus of Nazara. 6 vols.
Baur's Paul, his Life and Work. 2 vols.
Baur's Church History of the First Three Centuries. 2 vols.
Kuenen. The Religion of Israel. 3 vols.
Ewald. Prophets of the Old Testament. 5 vols.
Ewald's Commentary on the Psalms. 2 vols.
Ewald. Book of Job.
Bleek, on the Apocalypse.
Zeller, on the Acts of the Apostles. 2 vols.
Hausrath's History of the New Testament Times. 2 vols.
Pfleiderer's Paulinism. 2 vols.
Reville's Prolegomena of the History of Religions.
Schrader's The Cuneiform Inscriptions and the Old Testament. 2 vols.
Pfleiderer's Philosophy of Religion. 4 vols.

Theological Translation Fund—*(continued)*.

All new Subscribers may purchase any of the previous volumes at 7s. instead of 10s. 6d. per volume.

A selection of six or more volumes from the list may also be had at the Subscribers price, or 7s. per volume.

In the Press.
   Schrader's Cuneiform Inscriptions, Vol. II.
   Pfleiderer's Philosophy of Religion, Vol. II.

Vickers (J.) The History of Herod; or, Another Look at a Man emerging from Twenty Centuries of Calumny. 388 pp. Crown 8vo, cloth. 6s.

What I have taught my Children. By a Member of the Theistic Church. 12mo, cloth. 2s. 6d.

Williams (Dr. Rowland) The Hebrew Prophets. Translated afresh and illustrated for English Readers. 2 vols. 8vo, cloth. 22s. 6d.

Zeller (Dr. E.) The Contents and Origin of the Acts of the Apostles, critically investigated. Preceded by Dr. FR. OVERBECK's Introduction to the Acts of the Apostles from De Wette's Handbook. Translated by JOSEPH DARE. 2 vols. 8vo, cloth. 21s.

—— Vide Theological Translation Fund Library.

PAMPHLETS.

Athanasian Creed. Two Prize Essays. By C. Peabody and C. S. Kenny. 1s.
Beard (C.) William Ellery Channing. In Memoriam. A Sermon. 12mo. 6d.
Beard (C.) The Kingdom of God. A Sermon. 6d.
Beard (C.) The House of God, and two Sermons by Rev. R. A. Armstrong. 1s.
Butler's Analogy : A Lay Argument. By a Lancashire Manufacturer. 1s.
Hopgood (Jas.) Disestablishment and Disendowment of the Church of England. 6d.
Hopgood (Jas.) An Attempt to Define Unitarian Christianity. 6d.
Howe (Rev. C.) The Athanasian Creed. Two Discourses. 1s.
Jesus of Nazareth and his Contemporaries. 1s.
Journey to Emmaus. By a Modern Traveller. 2s.
Lisle (L.) The Two Tests : the Supernatural Claims of Christianity tried by two of its own Rules. Cloth. 1s. 6d.
Marriage of Cana, as read by a Layman. 6d.
Martineau (Rev. Dr. James) New Affinities of Faith ; a Plea for free Christian Union. 12mo. 1s.
Must God Annihilate the Wicked ? A Reply to Dr. Jos. Parker. 1s.
Reasonable Faith, A, the Want of our Age. 1s.
Savage (Rev. M. J.) Herbert Spencer : his Influence on Religion and Morality. 6d.
Sharpe (S.) Journeys and Epistles of the Apostle Paul. 1s. 6d.
Sidgwick (H.) The Ethics of Conformity and Subscription. 1s.
Tayler (Rev. J. J.) Christianity : What is it ? and What has it done ? 1s.

WILLIAMS AND NORGATE,
14, HENRIETTA STREET, COVENT GARDEN, LONDON;
AND 20, SOUTH FREDERICK STREET, EDINBURGH.

14, Henrietta Street, Covent Garden, London;
20, South Frederick Street, Edinburgh.

CATALOGUE OF SOME WORKS

PUBLISHED BY

WILLIAMS AND NORGATE.

Beard (Rev. Chas.) Port Royal, a Contribution to the History of Religion and Literature in France. Cheaper Edition. 2 vols. Crown 8vo. 12s

Bopp's Comparative Grammar of the Sanscrit, Zend, Greek, Latin, Lithuanian, Gothic, German, and Slavonic Languages. Translated by E. B. Eastwick. Fourth Edition. 3 vols. 8vo. cloth 31s 6d

Brewster. The Theories of Anarchy and of Law: A Midnight Debate. By H. B. Brewster, Esq. Crown 8vo. parchment 5s

Christ (The) and the Fathers, or the Reformers of the Roman Empire; being a Critical Analysis of the religious thoughts and opinion derived from their lives and letters, as well as from the Latin and Greek Fathers of the Eastern and Western Empires until the Nicene Council, with a Brief Sketch of the Continuation of Christianity until the Present Day in accordance with the Comparative Method of Historical Science. By an Historical Scientist. 8vo. cloth 7s 6d

Cobbe (Miss F. P.) The Hopes of the Human Race, Hereafter and Here. Essays on the Life after Death. With a Preface having special reference to Mr. Mill's Essay on Religion. Second Edition. Crown 8vo. cloth 5s

Cobbe (Miss F. P.) Darwinism in Morals, and (13) other Essays. (Religion in Childhood, Unconscious Cerebration, Dreams, the Devil, Auricular Confession, &c. &c.) 400 pp. 8vo. cloth (pub. at 10s) 5s

Cobbe (Miss F. P.) The Duties of Women. A Course of Lectures delivered in London and Clifton. Second Edition. Crown 8vo. cloth 5s

Cobbe (Miss F. P.) The Peak in Darien, and other Riddles of Life and Death. Crown 8vo. cloth 7s 6d

Cobbe (Miss F. P.) A Faithless World. With Additions and a
Preface. 8vo. cloth   2s 6d

Cobbe (Miss F. P.) Broken Lights. An Inquiry into the Present
Condition and Future Prospects of Religious Faith. Third Edition. Crown
8vo. cloth   5s

Cobbe (Miss F. P.) Dawning Lights. An Inquiry concerning the
Secular Results of the New Reformation. 8vo. cloth   5s

Cobbe (Miss F. P.) Alone to the Alone. Prayers for Theists, by
several Contributors. Third Edition. Crown 8vo. cloth, gilt edges   5s

Echoes of Holy Thoughts: arranged as Private Meditations before a
First Communion. Second Edition, with a Preface by the Rev. J. HAMILTON
THOM, of Liverpool. Printed with red lines. Crown 8vo. cloth   2s 6d

Evolution of Christianity, The. By CHARLES GILL. Second Edition,
with Dissertations in answer to Criticism. 8vo. cloth   12s

Gould (S. Baring) Lost and Hostile Gospels. An Account of the
Toledoth Jesher, two Hebrew Gospels circulating in the Middle Ages, and
extant Fragments of the Gospels of the First Three Centuries of Petrine and
Pauline Origin. By the Rev. S. BARING GOULD. Crown 8vo. cloth.   7s 6d

Jones (Rev. R. Crompton) Hymns of Duty and Faith, selected and
arranged. Second Edition. 247 pp. Foolscap 8vo. cloth   3s 6d

Mackay (R. W.) Sketch of the Rise and Progress of Christianity.
8vo. cloth   (pub. at 10s 6d) 6s

Mind: a Quarterly Review of Psychology and Philosophy. Contributions by Mr. Herbert Spencer, Professor Bain, Mr. Henry Sidgwick, Mr.
Shadworth H. Hodgson, Professor Flint, Mr. James Sully, the Rev. John
Venn, the Editor (Professor Croom Robertson), and others. Vols. I. to XII.,
1876-87, each 12s. Cloth, 13s   12s per annum, post free

Oldenberg (Prof. H.) Buddha: his Life, his Doctrine, his Order.
Translated by WILLIAM HOEY, M.A., D.LIT., Member of the Royal Asiatic
Society, Asiatic Society of Bengal, &c., of Her Majesty's Bengal Civil Service.
Cloth, gilt   18s

www.ingramcontent.com/pod-product-compliance
Lightning Source LLC
Chambersburg PA
CBHW020810230426
43666CB00007B/940